Apple Watcn
SENIORS GUIDE

The Most User-Friendly Seniors and Beginners Manual to Learning Apple Watch's Essential Features. Includes Pictures,

Simple Explanations and the Best Tips and Tricks!

VIN MAYER

Table of Contents

Scroll to the end and scan the QR CODE to download your FREE PDF

INTRODUCTION

The Apple Watch, manufactured by the renowned technology company Apple Inc., is an innovative smartwatch series that combines the convenience of a watch with the powerful features of an electronic device. This wearable device has been designed to offer much more than just a tool to check the time. Its sleek design and wide range of features make it an ideal companion for everyday life, offering a highly customizable experience and a set of applications that can greatly improve users' productivity, well-being, and enjoyment. In this introduction, we'll explore the different features and possibilities offered by the Apple Watch, opening the door to a world of connectivity, health tracking, and personalized style.

PUT YOURSELF TO THE TEST

The Apple Watch Ultra is designed for outdoor enthusiasts, with an Action button for quick access to information and emergency assistance. Customize the Modular Ultra watch face for different tasks. The unique action button can be customized for various functions. It is durable with a titanium case and water resistance up to 100 meters. Night mode improves visibility, and there's a siren for emergencies. Check out resources for customization and detailed features.

ADOPT HEALTHIER HABITS

Use Apple Watch Ultra to reach your fitness goals. Track your daily activities, set goals, and get notified when you reach your goals. Start workouts using the Action button or the Workout app and customize the workout view. For cycling, connect Bluetooth accessories for additional metrics. Track your progress over time with the Trends feature in the Fitness app. Explore resources for more details on using Apple Watch Ultra for fitness.

STAY IN TOUCH WITH THOSE YOU LOVE

Stay effortlessly connected with Apple Watch Ultra. Send messages using Siri, make calls, share your location, and share photos right from your wrist. The Ultra is designed to last and perform, with an action button for streamlined interactions and features like altimeters, depth gauges, and precision GPS for outdoor adventures. Explore the resources for more details on these features.

APPLE WATCH ULTRA: BUILT FOR ON-THE-GO TASKS

Apple Watch Ultra, the most rugged of the Apple Watch series, provides essential data for your outdoor activities such as hiking, running, and diving. It simplifies device operations through the convenient Action button, ensuring visibility during nighttime workouts. In addition, it has the ability to emit a loud and intermittent sound in case assistance is needed.

CONNECT THE WATCH FACE TO WHAT YOU'RE DOING

Customize the Modular Ultra watch face on your Apple Watch Ultra to display the information that's most relevant to your needs. Start by going to the Watch app on your iPhone, then go to the Watch Face Gallery. Swipe up to select the Modular Ultra watch face and proceed to choose the complications that best align with your planned activities, whether it's running, hiking, or diving.

LET'S START WITH SOME ACTION

The Apple Watch Ultra is distinguished by a unique feature not found in other Apple Watch models: the international orange Action button, located on the opposite side of the Digital Crown and side button. You have the flexibility to customize this Action key to perform a variety of functions, such as starting a workout or marking a compass waypoint with a single press. If you didn't set up the Action button during the initial pairing of your Apple Watch Ultra with your iPhone, simply go to the Settings app on your Apple Watch Ultra, tap "Action Button," and select your preferred action.

EXCEPTIONALLY DURABLE COMPARED TO ITS COUNTERPARTS

The Apple Watch Ultra boasts a titanium case that resists corrosion, a flat sapphire crystal dial, advanced protection for the raised Digital Crown, and water resistance up to 100 meters. This makes it the perfect companion for your next backpacking expedition, your next triathlon event, or even a deep-sea dive in the ocean.3

IMPROVES NIGHT-TIME VISIBILITY

To make sure you can easily see your watch at night, both the "Modular Ultra" and Wayfinder watch faces will automatically switch to a red color scheme during the night hours. To enable this feature, press and hold one of the watch faces, enter the Edit option, scroll down to find Night Mode, and then choose the Automatic setting.

GET HELP WHEN YOU NEED IT

The Apple Watch Ultra comes with a siren that can be used to alert nearby people in an emergency. If you find yourself in an unexpected situation, press and hold the side button, then slide the siren slider to the right to activate it. Alternatively, you can also activate the siren by pressing and holding the Action button.

STAY ACTIVE WITH APPLE WATCH ULTRA

Apple Watch Ultra not only tracks your physical activity and workout routines, but also motivates you to stay active through friendly reminders and engaging challenges.

STAY ON TOP OF KEY HEALTH INFORMATION

Apple Watch Ultra can help you reach your sleep goals, track vital data related to your heart health, track your emotional well-being and moods, document your medication schedule, and supervise your menstrual cycle.

SLEEP PLAYS A CRUCIAL ROLE IN YOUR WELL-BEING

With the Sleep app on Apple Watch Ultra, you can establish a bedtime routine, set a sleep duration goal, and drill down into your recent sleep history. In addition, you will get information about your sleep stages, including REM, medium and deep sleep, along with the number of awakenings you experienced. While you sleep, Apple Watch Ultra diligently monitors key metrics such as blood oxygen levels, heart rate, sleep duration, respiratory rate, and wrist temperature. To get started, simply launch the Sleep app on your Apple Watch Ultra and follow the intuitive on-screen instructions. So, make it a habit to wear your Apple Watch Ultra even before you go to sleep and let your device take care of the rest.

STAY INFORMED ABOUT HEART HEALTH

On your Apple Watch Ultra, you have the option to turn on Heart Rate app notifications, which will keep you informed of significant changes in your heart rate. These notifications can alert you when your heart rate is unusually high or low, and they can also alert you to irregular heart rhythms that may indicate the presence of atrial fibrillation (AFib). If you have a previous diagnosis of atrial fibrillation, you can enable the "History of Atrial Fibrillation" feature to receive estimates of how often your heart has experienced arrhythmia. In addition, you can choose to receive notifications related to low cardiovascular tone.

MANAGE YOUR MEDICATIONS EFFECTIVELY

The Medication app is a valuable tool to help you stay organized with your medications, vitamins, and supplements. All you have to do is include your medications in the health app on your iPhone and then log them to your Apple Watch Ultra for seamless tracking and management.

DOCUMENT YOUR EMOTIONAL STATE

In addition to facilitating mindful breathing exercises and fostering moments of introspection, the Mindfulness app helps cultivate emotional awareness and resilience by acknowledging one's feelings. To get started, log in to the Mindfulness app and select "Mood." From there, you can record your emotions and moods at various times of the day.

TRACK YOUR MENSTRUAL CYCLE

Use the "Cycle Tracker" feature to enter daily details about your menstrual cycle. Apple Watch Ultra leverages this data to provide insights and predictions about your fertility cycle and window. In addition to manually entered information, Cycle Tracker can improve its predictions by incorporating heart rate data. If you constantly wear Apple Watch Ultra while sleeping, the app can also consider your wrist temperature to further refine your cycle predictions and provide retrospective estimates of ovulation.

Please note that retrospective ovulation estimates may not be accessible in all regions.

1 - SET UP AND ESTABLISH THE CONNECTION BETWEEN YOUR IPHONE AND APPLE WATCH ULTRA

To use your Apple Watch Ultra, it's essential to establish a connection with your iPhone. Setup assistants on both iPhone and Apple Watch Ultra work together to guide you through the pairing and setup process.

If you're having trouble locating your Apple Watch Ultra or iPhone, you have the option to use VoiceOver or Zoom, even during initial setup. For step-by-step steps about setting up Apple Watch Ultra with VoiceOver or using Zoom on your device, see the resources provided.

REQUIREMENTS FOR APPLE WATCH ULTRA WITH WATCHOS 10

To use your Apple Watch Ultra with watchOS 10, it's imperative to pair it with an iPhone Xs or a newer model, running on iOS 17 or later. This pairing ensures seamless functionality between the two devices.

BEFORE YOU START THE PROCESS

- Before embarking on the setup journey, it's crucial to make sure your iPhone is running the latest iOS version. To achieve this, simply go to the Settings app on your iPhone, select General, and then tap Software Update.

- Also, make sure that your iPhone has Bluetooth enabled and is connected to a Wi-Fi network or cellular network. You can check this by swiping down from the top right corner of your iPhone screen to access the Control Center. Make sure the Bluetooth and Wi-Fi (or cellular) buttons are both on, indicating a successful connection.

STEP 1: TURN ON AND ESTABLISH A CONNECTION WITH APPLE WATCH ULTRA

1. Start by wearing your Apple Watch Ultra. Adjust the strap to ensure it fits comfortably and securely on your wrist, striking the right balance between snug and tight. For guidance on how to replace the band on your Apple Watch Ultra, see the instructions for how to remove, change, and fasten your Apple Watch bands.
2. To activate Apple Watch Ultra, press and hold the side button until the Apple logo becomes visible. If your Apple Watch Ultra won't turn on, you might need to charge it.
3. Now, bring your iPhone close to the Apple Watch Ultra and wait patiently for the Apple Watch pairing screen to appear on your iPhone. Once it appears, tap on the "Continue" option. Alternatively, you can choose to launch the Watch app on your iPhone and then select "Pair a New Apple Watch" to start the pairing process.
4. Choose the "Set Up for Me" option.
5. When prompted, align your iPhone so that your Apple Watch Ultra is visible within the Watch app interface. This action will make it easier to pair the two devices.

STEP 2: SET UP APPLE WATCH ULTRA

1. If this is your initial experience with an Apple Watch Ultra, tap Set Up Apple Watch and then follow the on-screen instructions provided by both your iPhone and Apple Watch Ultra to finalize the setup. For those who have previously set up another Apple Watch with their iPhone, you will encounter the choice "Make this device your new Apple Watch". Select "Apps & Data" and "Settings" to preview the quick setup setup for your new Apple Watch. Tap "Continue" to proceed with the suggested configuration. If you prefer to customize the settings for your Apple Watch differently, opt for "Customize Settings." You can also choose a backup from a previous Apple Watch to restore.

Alternatively, selecting "Set Up as New Apple Watch" gives you full customization of your new device's settings.

2. Follow the on-screen instructions to set the following preferences:
   - Provide your Apple ID and password.
   - Establish a passcode, which can be a standard four-digit code or a more secure six-digit code.
   - Customize the text size to your liking. Optionally, enter personal data such as your date of birth and height, which will be used for fitness and health purposes. Also, select the Health notifications you want to receive.

   Note that you can change these settings later after you've successfully set up your Apple Watch Ultra.

STEP 3: TURN ON CELLULAR SERVICES

You have the option to enable cellular services for your Apple Watch Ultra during the initial setup. Alternatively, you can activate this feature later through the Watch app on your iPhone. For step-by-step instructions, see the guide on setting up and using cellular services on Apple Watch Ultra.

Keep in mind that cellular service availability may vary depending on your location.

STEP 4: KEEP DEVICES NEARBY WHILE SYNCING

After the pairing process is complete, the watch face will appear on your Apple Watch Ultra and your device will be ready to use.

While the syncing process is ongoing, you can access more details about your Apple Watch Ultra by tapping "Discover Apple Watch." Here, you can explore the latest features, access helpful Apple Watch tips, and refer to this user guide, all right from your iPhone. Once your Apple Watch Ultra is fully set up, you can access this information by opening the Watch app on your iPhone and selecting the "Discover" tab.

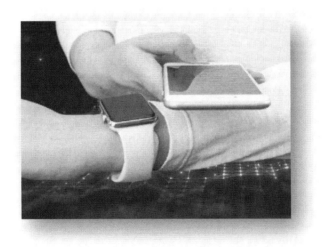

ARE YOU HAVING TROUBLE WITH THE PAIRING PROCESS?

- If you encounter a watch face while trying to pair, it means that your Apple Watch Ultra is already connected to an iPhone. In this case, you will need to erase all data and reset the settings on your Apple Watch Ultra.

- If the camera doesn't start the pairing process, you can select "Pair Apple Watch Manually" located at the bottom of your iPhone screen and follow the instructions provided on the screen. If you're having trouble pairing your Apple Watch Ultra with your iPhone, see the Apple Support article titled "If your Apple Watch isn't connected or paired with your iPhone" for more help.

SET UP MULTIPLE APPLE WATCHES
Multiple Apple Watches can be connected to your iPhone and seamlessly switch between them as needed.

PAIR MULTIPLE APPLE WATCHES
To pair an additional Apple Watch, simply repeat the same process you did for the first one. Make sure your iPhone is in close proximity to your Apple Watch, wait for the pairing screen to appear on your iPhone, and then tap Pair. Alternatively, you can follow these steps:
1. Open the Watch app on your iPhone.
2. Tap My Watch, then choose All Apple Watches at the top of the screen.
3. Select Add Apple Watch, then proceed to follow the onscreen instructions. For more information, see the Apple Support article titled "Use Apple Watch More with iPhone."

QUICKLY SWITCH TO ANOTHER APPLE WATCH
Your iPhone will intelligently identify the paired Apple Watch you're wearing and automatically establish a connection. If you switch to another Apple Watch, simply lift your wrist.
However, if you'd rather manually select the Apple Watch you want to connect to, follow these steps:

1. Launch the Watch app on your iPhone.
2. Tap My Watch, then select All Apple Watches at the top of the screen.
3. Disable "Auto-Connect" and choose the desired Apple Watch from the list.

To check if your Apple Watch is connected to your iPhone, access the Control Center by pressing the side button and look for the "Connected" status icon.

PAIR APPLE WATCH ULTRA WITH ANOTHER IPHONE
If you initially paired your Apple Watch Ultra with your previous iPhone and now want to pair it with a new one, follow these steps:
1. Use iCloud backup to create a backup of your current iPhone, which is currently paired with your Apple Watch Ultra (refer to your iPhone's User Guide for step-by-step instructions).
2. Set up your new iPhone. On the "Apps & Data" screen during the setup process, choose to restore from an iCloud backup and choose the most recent backup.
3. Continue setting up your iPhone, and when prompted, select the option to use Apple Watch Ultra with your new iPhone.

4. After you've finished setting up your iPhone, you'll need to pair your Apple Watch Ultra with your new device. Confirm this action by tapping "OK" on your Apple Watch, then enter the code provided. For more guidance, see the Apple Support article titled "How to pair your Apple Watch with a new iPhone."

SELECT AN ACTION FOR THE APPLE WATCH ULTRA ACTION BUTTON

When you set up your Apple Watch Ultra, you'll be asked to designate a feature for the Action button. There are several options available, including:

ACTION	PRESSURE
FORMATION	-First press: Open the Workout app or start a workout -Second pressure: depends on the workout you choose
CHRONOMETER	-First press: start -Second press: mark the lap
WAYPOINT	Setting a waypoint compass
RETRACE YOUR STEPS	Save the itinerary file
IMMERSION	Start a dive
TORCH	-First press: On -Second press: deactivate
QUICK COMMAND	Start of the shortcut

Some actions provide additional options when you press both the Action key and the Side key at the same time. You have the flexibility to change the function of the Action key after the initial setup. To do this, go to the Settings app on your Apple Watch and go to the Action button settings.

CHARGE APPLE WATCH ULTRA

PREPARE THE CHARGER

1. Find a well-ventilated location and place the charger or charging cable on a flat surface.
2. Apple Watch Ultra comes with the USB-C Magnetic Fast Charging Cable that has a USB-C connector. Alternatively, you can use a MagSafe Duo charger or the Apple Watch Magnetic Charging Dock (available separately).
3. Connect the charging cable to the power adapter (sold separately).
4. Plug the power adapter into a power outlet.

Please note that fast charging requires an 18W or higher USB-C power adapter. For more details, see the Apple Support article on fast charging your Apple Watch.
Note: Fast charging availability may vary by region.

START THE CHARGING PROCESS FOR APPLE WATCH ULTRA

Gently connect the Apple Watch USB-C Magnetic Fast Charging Cable to the back of your Apple Watch Ultra. The charging cable has a concave design that securely attaches to the back of Apple Watch Ultra using a magnetic connection, ensuring proper alignment.

When charging begins, Apple Watch Ultra makes an audible sound (unless it's in silent mode) and a charging icon appears on the watch face. This icon is red when Apple Watch Ultra requires charging and turns green when the device is actively charging. When Apple Watch Ultra is in Low Power Mode, the charging icon appears in yellow.

You have the option to charge Apple Watch Ultra while it's lying horizontally with the band open or by placing it on its side.

If you're using the Magnetic Dock to charge your Apple Watch or MagSafe Power Duo: Place your Apple Watch Ultra on the dock.

In case the battery level is extremely low: You may see an image of the Apple Watch Magnetic to USB-C Fast Charger Cable or the Apple Watch Magnetic Charging Cable along with the low battery symbol on the screen. For more help, see the Apple Support article titled "If your Apple Watch won't charge or turn on."

MONITOR THE REMAINING BATTERY POWER

For a quick check of the remaining battery power, simply press the side button to enter the Control Center. If you want even faster access to the state of charge, consider adding a battery complication directly to the watch face.

PRESERVES BATTERY LIFE

To conserve battery power, consider turning on the "Low Power Mode". When Power Saver is on, it disables the "Always On" screen setting, background heart rate monitoring, blood oxygen measurement, and heart rate notifications. In this mode, other notifications may be delayed, emergency alerts may not arrive, and some cellular and Wi-Fi connections will be limited. The cellular network remains off until you need to, such as when you're streaming music or need to send a message.

Keep in mind that Low Power Mode will automatically turn off once the battery reaches 80% charge.

Follow these steps:
1. Press the side button to access the Control Center.
2. Tap the battery percentage.
3. Enable Power Saving Mode.
4. To confirm, scroll down and turn on the option.
5. If you want, tap "Activate for" and select the duration: "On for 1 day", "On for 2 days", or "On for 3 days".

RECOMMEND: If you've connected a battery-powered device, such as AirPods, to your Apple Watch Ultra via Bluetooth, go to Control Center and tap the battery percentage. Then, use the Digital Crown to view the remaining charge.

In addition, when the battery level drops to 10% or less, Apple Watch Ultra will notify you and offer you the option to turn on Low Power Mode.

CHECK THE ELAPSED TIME SINCE THE LAST CHARGE

Launch the Settings app on your Apple Watch Ultra.
Select Battery.
The Battery screen will display the remaining percentage, a graph illustrating recent charging events, and details about the last time the battery was charged.

CHECK THE CONDITION OF THE BATTERY

Here's how to determine the battery capacity of your Apple Watch Ultra compared to when it was new:
1. Launch the Settings app on your Apple Watch Ultra.
2. Tap Battery, then choose Battery Health.

Apple Watch Ultra will send you notifications if your battery capacity is extremely low and give you options to manage your service.

MAXIMIZE BATTERY LIFE

To extend the battery life of Apple Watch Ultra, it uses on-device machine learning to understand your daily charging habits. It delays charging by more than 80% until it is needed for usage.

Here's how to enable this feature:
1. Go to the Settings app on your Apple Watch Ultra.
2. Tap Battery, then choose Battery Health.
3. Turn on the optimized charge limit.

PREVENT BACKGROUND APP UPDATES

When you switch to a new app on Apple Watch Ultra, the old app doesn't stay open and doesn't use system resources. However, it may continue to refresh its content in the background, which can drain battery power.
To optimize battery life, you can disable this background app refresh feature:
1. Open the Settings app on your Apple Watch Ultra.
2. Go to General > "Refresh Background Apps."
3. Turn off background app refresh to stop all background apps from refreshing. Alternatively, scroll through the list and turn off the update for specific apps individually.

Keep in mind that apps with complications on the current watch face will continue to update, even if their background refresh option is disabled.

LOCK OR UNLOCK APPLE WATCH ULTRA
UNLOCKING APPLE WATCH ULTRA

You can manually unlock your Apple Watch Ultra by entering your passcode, or you can set it up to unlock automatically when you unlock your iPhone.
1. Enter your passcode: To manually unlock your Apple Watch Ultra, activate your device, then enter your passcode.

2. Unlock Apple Watch Ultra with iPhone: Open the Watch app on your iPhone, tap "My Watch," select "Passcode," and enable "Unlock with iPhone."

Your iPhone must be within the standard Bluetooth range, about 10 meters, of your Apple Watch Ultra to enable auto-unlock. If Bluetooth isn't enabled on your Apple Watch Ultra, you can enter the passcode on your watch to unlock it.

Tip: We recommend using different passcodes for Apple Watch Ultra and iPhone for added security.

CHANGING THE PASSCODE

You can change the passcode you initially set for your Apple Watch Ultra by following these steps:

Your Apple Watch Ultra:
1. Open the Settings app.
2. Tocca "Passcode".
3. Select "Change Passcode" and follow the on-screen instructions.

Alternatively, you can change the passcode using your iPhone:
1. Open the Watch app on your iPhone.
2. Tocca "Apple Watch".
3. Choose "Passcode".
4. Select "Change Passcode" and follow the on-screen instructions.

Tip: If you want to use a passcode longer than four digits, go to the Settings app on your Apple Watch Ultra, tap Passcode, and turn off Simple Passcode.

DISABLING THE PASSCODE

To turn off passcode on your Apple Watch Ultra, follow these steps:

Your Apple Watch Ultra:
1. Launch the Settings app.
2. Select "Passcode."
3. Tap "Disable Passcode."

Alternatively, you can disable the passcode using your iPhone:
1. Open the Watch app on your iPhone.
2. Tocca "Apple Watch".
3. Choose "Passcode".
4. Select "Disable Passcode."

Keep in mind that disabling the passcode will result in the loss of some features. For example, you won't be able to use Apple Pay or unlock your Mac with Apple Watch Ultra.

USING A SIMPLE PASSCODE OR DISABLING

Note that the options to use a simple passcode or disable it may not be accessible if the synced iPhone is under the management of an organization, such as a business or educational institution. In these cases, we recommend that you contact your organization's IT administrator for further assistance.

APPLE WATCH ULTRA AUTO-LOCK

By default, Apple Watch Ultra is set to automatically lock when not worn on your wrist. If you want to adjust your wrist detection settings, you can follow the steps outlined below:

1. Go to the Settings app on your Apple Watch Ultra.
2. Select "Passcode," then turn pulse detection on or off.

Note that disabling wrist tracking will affect the following functions of your Apple Watch Ultra:

- When using Apple Pay, you'll need to enter the code when you double-click the side button to authorize a payment.
- Some activity measurements may not be available.
- Heart rate monitoring and notifications will be turned off.
- Apple Watch Ultra won't lock and will automatically unlock.
- In the event of a significant fall, Apple Watch Ultra won't automatically make an emergency call, even if it detects the fall.

MANUALLY LOCK APPLE WATCH ULTRA

Note that to manually lock your Apple Watch Ultra, you must first disable wrist tracking. To do this, follow these steps:

1. Open the Settings app on your Apple Watch Ultra.
2. Tap Passcode, then turn off Wrist Detection.

After disabling wrist tracking, you can manually lock your Apple Watch Ultra by following these steps:

1. Press the side button to access the Control Center.
2. Tap the "Block" button.

After that, when you use your Apple Watch Ultra again, you will be required to enter your passcode.

IN CASE YOU FORGET YOUR PASSCODE

If you happen to forget your Apple Watch Ultra passcode, you'll need to erase your device. There are two ways to do this:

1. Unpair your Apple Watch Ultra from your iPhone, which will reset your Apple Watch settings and passcode. After that, you can proceed to pair again.
2. Perform a reset on your Apple Watch Ultra and then pair it with your iPhone again.

Erase Apple Watch Ultra after 10 incorrect unlock attempts.

To protect your watch's data if it's lost or stolen, you can set up your Apple Watch Ultra to erase your watch's data after 10 consecutive failed attempts to enter your passcode.

Here's how to enable this feature:

1. Open the Settings app on your Apple Watch Ultra.
2. Tap "Passcode," then turn on the "Clear Data" option.

ADJUSTING THE LANGUAGE AND ORIENTATION OF APPLE WATCH ULTRA
SELECT YOUR PREFERRED LANGUAGE OR COUNTRY

If you've set up your iPhone with multiple languages, you can easily select the language displayed on your Apple Watch Ultra. Here's how to do it:

1. Launch the Watch app on your iPhone.
2. Tap My Watch, then go to General > Language & Region.

3. Tap "Customize" and choose your preferred language from the list.
4. To add another language, select "Add Language" and choose the language you want to include.

Please note that in languages with grammatical genders, you can specify whether you prefer the masculine, feminine, or neuter form to be used throughout the system.

Change the orientation of your wrist or reverse the orientation of your Digital Crown

If you want to wear Apple Watch Ultra on your alternate wrist or prefer the Digital Crown on the opposite side, you can customize the orientation settings to make sure your watch responds appropriately to wrist movements and crown rotations.

Here's how to adjust these settings:

1. Open the Settings app on your Apple Watch Ultra.
2. Go to "General" > "Orientation".

Alternatively, you can achieve the same using the Watch app on your iPhone. Just tap "My Watch," navigate to "General," and then select "Orientation."

STATUS ICONS ON APPLE WATCH ULTRA

●	You have an unread notification. Swipe down on the watch face to read it.
⚡	Apple Watch Ultra is charging.
⚡	The battery in your Apple Watch Ultra is low.
○	The "Power Saver" mode is on.
🔒	Apple Watch Ultra is locked. Tap to enter the code and unlock.
💧	Lock when in the water" is on and the screen does not respond to touches. Press and rotate the Digital Crown.
🌙	The "Do Not Disturb" function is turned on. Calls and alerts will be silent and will not illuminate the screen; Alarms will still be active
👤	Personal Focus is turned on.
💼	The Work Focus is turned on.
🛏	Full sleep immersion is activated.
✈	Airplane mode is turned on. The wireless connection is not active, but features that do not use the wireless connection are still available.
🏃	Training is ongoing
✕	Apple Watch Ultra is connected to a cellular network
▯	People Watch Ultra has disconnected from the paired iPhone. This occurs when your Apple Watch Ultra isn't near your iPhone or when Airplane mode is turned on.
▯	Apple Watch Ultra is connected to the iPhone it's paired with.
➤	An app on Apple Watch Ultra uses location tracking
📶	Apple Watch Ultra is connected to a known Wi-Fi network.
⋮	There is wireless an active activity or process.
🎤	The microphone is active.

.ıll	Apple Watch Ultra is connected to a cellular network. The number of green bars indicates the signal strength.
📷	You have made yourself available to be reached on Walkie-Talkie. Tap the icon to open the Walkie-Talkie app.

USE CONTROL CENTER ON APPLE WATCH ULTRA

Control Center provides access to features such as battery check, Apple Watch Ultra muting, theater mode activation, flashlight use, airplane mode activation, entertainment mode activation, and more.

ACCESS CONTROL CENTER

Access Control Center by pressing the side button, and to close Control Center, move your wrist away from the screen or press the side button again while it's open.

TO REVIEW THE STATUS OF CONTROL CENTER

Small symbols located in the upper section of the Control Center provide information about the status of specific settings. These icons convey information about things like whether your Apple Watch Ultra is connected to cellular networks, whether an app uses your location, and how enabled features like Do Not Disturb have been activated.

To access these status icons, simply press the side button to open the Control Center. For more information, you can tap the icons to see more details.

ADJUST THE LAYOUT OF THE CONTROL CENTER TO SUIT YOUR PREFERENCES

To rearrange the buttons within Control Center, follow these steps:
1. Open Control Center by pressing the side button.

2. Scroll to the bottom of Control Center, then select "Edit."
3. Press and hold a button, then move it to the desired location.
4. Tap "Done" when you're done arranging the buttons.

DELETE THE CONTROL CENTER BUTTONS
You can delete buttons in Control Center by following these steps:
1. Open Control Center by pressing the side button.
2. Scroll to the bottom and tap Edit.
3. Tap the Delete button in the corner of the button you want to remove.
4. Tap Done when you're done.

To restore a removed button, go to Control Center, tap Edit, and select the "Added" button in the corner of the button you want to restore. Tap Done when you're done.

ENABLE AIRPLANE MODE
Some airlines allow Apple Watch Ultra (and iPhone) to be used in airplane mode. By default, turning on Airplane Mode disables Wi-Fi and cellular connections but keeps Bluetooth on. You can customize the settings that are enabled or disabled when you turn on airplane mode.

To turn on Airplane mode on your Apple Watch Ultra, press the side button to open Control Center and select the Airplane button.

Give Siri a try: Say "turn on airplane mode."

You can enable Airplane mode on both Apple Watch Ultra and iPhone at the same time. Open the Watch app on your iPhone, tap My Watch, go to General > Airplane, and enable iPhone Mirroring. When your iPhone and Apple Watch Ultra are within Bluetooth range (about 10 meters), turning on Airplane mode on one device will also activate it for the other.

To customize which settings are turned on or off when Airplane mode is enabled, follow these steps on your Apple Watch Ultra: Open the Settings app, tap Airplane mode, and choose whether to enable or disable Wi-Fi or Bluetooth by default when you turn on Airplane mode.

If you want to enable or disable Wi-Fi or Bluetooth separately while Airplane Mode is on on your Apple Watch Ultra, open the Settings app, then tap Wi-Fi or Bluetooth.

You'll see the airplane mode icon at the top of the screen when airplane mode is on. Keep in mind that even with iPhone mirroring enabled, you'll need to disable Airplane mode individually on both your iPhone and Apple Watch Ultra.

USE THE FLASHLIGHT FEATURE ON YOUR APPLE WATCH ULTRA
Turn on the flashlight on Apple Watch Ultra to illuminate locks in the dark, signal during night runs, or illuminate nearby objects without interrupting night vision.

To enable the flashlight, press the side button, enter the Control Center, and tap the flashlight icon. Swipe left to select between solid white light, flashing white light, or solid red light.

You can adjust the brightness by turning the Digital Crown up or down.

To turn off the flashlight, press the Digital Crown or side button, or swipe down from the top of the watch face.

DISCONNECT FROM WI-FI

In Control Center, you have the option to briefly disconnect from a Wi-Fi network, and if you have cellular service on your Apple Watch Ultra, use a cellular connection instead.

To achieve this, simply press the side button to open the Control Center, then select the Wi-Fi button.

Apple Watch Ultra briefly stops connecting to your Wi-Fi network, and if you have an active cellular plan, switches to cellular service when available. When you return to a known Wi-Fi area, Apple Watch Ultra will automatically reconnect to the network, unless you manually disconnected it using your iPhone.

To quickly access Wi-Fi settings on Apple Watch Ultra, simply press and hold the Wi-Fi button in Control Center.

TURN ON SILENT MODE

Press the side button, go to Control Center, and tap the Silent button.

Note that if your Apple Watch Ultra is charging, alarms and timers will continue to produce sounds despite silent mode being enabled.

Alternatively, you can go to the Watch app on your iPhone, select My Watch, go to Sounds & Haptics, and enable the Silent option.

As a helpful tip, when you receive a notification, you can quickly silence your Apple Watch Ultra by placing your palm on the watch screen for a minimum of three seconds. You will receive haptic feedback confirming once the sound has been muted. Make sure Cover to Mute is turned on on your Apple Watch Ultra by opening the Settings app, selecting Sounds & Haptics, and turning on Cover to Mute.

CHANGE THE SCREEN BRIGHTNESS, TEXT SIZE, AUDIO SETTINGS, AND HAPTIC FEEDBACK ON APPLE WATCH ULTRA TO YOUR PREFERENCES.

CUSTOMIZE THE SCREEN BRIGHTNESS AND TEXT SIZE TO YOUR LIKING ON APPLE WATCH ULTRA

Access the display and text settings on Apple Watch Ultra by opening the Settings app and navigating to Display & Brightness, where you can customize the brightness, text size, and enable bold text. Alternatively, you can make these adjustments on your iPhone through the Watch app.

CHANGE THE AUDIO SETTINGS

Go to the Ultra Settings app on your Apple Watch.

Select "Sounds & Haptics."

Adjust the volume by tapping the control or using the Digital Crown.

Alternatively, on your iPhone, launch the Watch app, go to Sounds & Haptics, and adjust the alert volume slider.

To minimize excessive sound levels from headphones connected to your Apple Watch Ultra, go to Sounds & Haptics > Hearing Health in the Settings app and turn on Loud Sounds.

CHANGE THE INTENSITY OF THE HAPTIC FEEDBACK VIBRATIONS

You can customize the intensity of haptic feedback used for notifications and alerts on Apple Watch Ultra.

1. Open the Settings app on your Apple Watch Ultra.
2. Go to Sounds & Haptics, then enable Haptic Alerts.
3. Select Default or Badges.

Alternatively, you can adjust this setting on your iPhone by opening the Watch app, tapping My Watch, selecting Sounds & Haptics, and choosing between Default and Badge.

TURN ON/OFF THE DIGITAL CROWN'S HAPTIC FEEDBACK

To enable or disable haptic feedback when scrolling with the Digital Crown on Apple Watch Ultra, follow these steps:

1. Open the Settings app on your Apple Watch Ultra.
2. Tap Sounds & Haptics.
3. Turn the Digital Crown's haptic feedback on or off.

You can also control system-wide haptic feedback settings via the same menu. Alternatively, you can make these adjustments using the Watch app on your iPhone.

USING HAPTIC TIME ON APPLE WATCH ULTRA

When Apple Watch Ultra is in silent mode, it can transmit the time using distinct touch patterns on the wrist. To enable this feature, follow these steps:

1. Open the Settings app on your Apple Watch Ultra.
2. Tap "Clock," scroll down, and select "Touch Time."
3. Turn on Haptics, then choose one of the settings: Digits, Concise, or Morse Code.
   - Numbers: Apple Watch Ultra will provide long haptic feedback every 10 hours, short feedback for every next hour, long feedback every 10 minutes, and short feedback for every minute thereafter.
   - Concise: Apple Watch Ultra will perform long haptic feedback every five hours, short feedback for the remaining hours, and long feedback every quarter of an hour.
   - Morse Code: Apple Watch Ultra will transmit the time using Morse code haptic feedback for each digit.

Alternatively, you can set up Haptic Time on your iPhone:

1. Open the Watch app on your iPhone.
2. Tap "My Watch," go to "Watch," and select "Haptic."
3. Turn on the feature.

Note: If haptic time is turned off, your Apple Watch Ultra might be set to announce the time acoustically. To use touch time, first go to "Settings" > "Clock" on your watch, and then enable "Silent Mode Control" under "Read Time."

USE SMART GALLERY TO AUTOMATICALLY DISPLAY WIDGETS WHEN NEEDED ON APPLE WATCH ULTRA

A smart collection includes widgets that intelligently adapt based on factors like time, location, and your activities. For example, in the morning, the Weather app shows the forecast, or when you're on the road, your tickets appear in Wallet.

GO TO THE SMART GALLERY

If you don't see the watch face, press the Digital Crown.
Scroll through the widgets by turning the Digital Crown.
Find the widget you want to use, then tap it to open the corresponding apps.
Tip: There's a widget at the bottom of the smart library that includes the Music, Workouts, and Messages apps. Tap an app to open it.

MANAGE WIDGETS ON APPLE WATCH ULTRA

Customize your Smart Gallery by adding, removing, or rearranging widgets. Swipe down from the watch face, touch and hold Smart Collection, and choose one of the following actions:
- Add a widget: Tap the "+" button, then select a widget or app from the "All apps" section. Some apps offer multiple widgets.
- Remove a widget: Tap the Delete button to remove a widget.
- Pin a widget: Use the Add button located to the right of the widget to pin it. Pinned widgets will appear below the last pinned widget in the Smart Collection. You can adjust the order by tapping the pin button next to each widget.

When you're done customizing your Smart Collection, tap "Done" to save your changes.

CHECK YOUR APPLE ID SETTINGS ON YOUR APPLE WATCH ULTRA.

You have the option to review and edit the details linked to your Apple ID. This includes changing contact information, changing your password, embedding a trusted phone number, and more.

REVIEW YOUR PERSONAL DATA

Go to settings on your Apple Watch Ultra. Tap [your name], then tap Personal Info. Perform actions:
- Edit your name by tapping on it and selecting First Name, Middle Name, or Last Name.
- Change your date of birth by selecting Birthday and entering a new date.
- Change your communication preferences for Apple News announcements, tips, and newsletters. You can turn on ads, app recommendations, music, TV, and more, or sign up for the Apple News newsletter.

MANAGE APPLE ID SECURITY AND PASSWORDS ON APPLE WATCH ULTRA

Open the Apple Watch Ultra Settings app, tap your name, then go to Sign in & Security. Here you can manage your Apple ID settings:
- Check and manage the phone numbers and email addresses associated with your Apple ID.
- Remove verified email addresses.
- Add new email addresses and phone numbers.
- Change your Apple ID password.
- Manage trusted phone numbers for two-factor authentication.
- Get verification codes for access on other devices or iCloud.com.
- Adjust Sign in with Apple settings for apps or websites.
- Hide your email address using a forwarding option.
- Check the status of your recovery key.

These actions allow you to maintain the security and functionality of your Apple ID on Apple Watch Ultra.

SIGN IN AND CONTROL YOUR SUBSCRIPTION SERVICES ON APPLE WATCH ULTRA.

Open the Settings app on your Apple Watch Ultra. Connect Apple Watch Ultra to your Wi-Fi network.
Tap [your name].
Tap Subscriptions to view your active and expired subscriptions.
You can tap a subscription to view its cost and validity or make changes to your subscription preferences.
To cancel a subscription, select "Cancel Subscription."
Note: Some subscriptions may require you to cancel through your iPhone.
To renew an expired subscription, select it and choose the plan you want, such as monthly or yearly.

USE SHORTCUTS ON APPLE WATCH ULTRA EFFICIENTLY

The Shortcuts app on Apple Watch Ultra makes it easy to get things done with a single tap. You can create shortcuts on your iPhone for tasks like getting directions home or creating a playlist of the top 25 songs. These shortcuts can be done through the Shortcuts app, the Action button, or added as complications to the watch face.
Keep in mind that not all iPhone shortcuts are compatible with Apple Watch Ultra.

ACTIVATE A SHORTCUT

Launch the Shortcuts app on your Apple Watch Ultra. Choose a shortcut.
Perform a shortcut with the Action button.
Customize the Action button on Apple Watch Ultra:
1. Go to settings on your Apple Watch Ultra.
2. Choose the Action button.
3. Set it up with a preferred shortcut.

Note that if you haven't set up any shortcuts on your iPhone, you won't see the option to assign one to the Action button.

INTEGRATE A SHORTCUT AS A COMPLICATION

Press and hold the knob, choose "Edit," swipe left on the complications screen, and select a shortcut from the available options.

EXPAND APPLE WATCH ULTRA SHORTCUT OPTIONS

Access other shortcut options on your iPhone:
1. Open the Shortcuts app.
2. Tap the More button (in the upper-right corner) of a shortcut.
3. On the shortcuts screen, tap the Info button, then enable Show on Apple Watch Ultra.

CONNECT APPLE WATCH ULTRA TO WI-FI

When you connect your Apple Watch Ultra to a Wi-Fi network, it gives you access to a variety of features, even if your iPhone isn't in range.

SELECT A WI-FI NETWORK

To select a Wi-Fi network on your Apple Watch Ultra, follow these steps:
1. Press the side button to open Control Center.
2. Press and hold the Wi-Fi button.
3. Tap the name of an available Wi-Fi network.

Note that Wi-Fi networks that are compatible with Apple Watch Ultra are those that support 802.11b/g/n at 2.4 GHz.

If the selected network requires a password, you can enter it using one of the following methods:
- Use the keyboard on your Apple Watch Ultra to enter your password (note that this feature may not be available in all languages).
- Use your finger to write characters on the screen and use the Digital Crown to select uppercase or lowercase characters.
- Tap the Password button, then choose a password from the list.
- Alternatively, you can use your iPhone's keyboard to enter the password.

After entering the password, tap "Sign In" to connect to the selected Wi-Fi network.

ENABLE PRIVATE NETWORK ADDRESS ON APPLE WATCH ULTRA FOR MORE PRIVACY

To improve privacy, Apple Watch Ultra uses a unique private network address called Media Access Control (MAC) on each connected Wi-Fi network. However, for networks that require identification or parental controls, you can disable this feature.
1. Open Control Center by pressing the side button.
2. Long press the Wi-Fi button and select the network.
3. Turn off Private Address.

Note: For added privacy, keep the "Private Address" option enabled on networks that support it. This reduces tracking on various Wi-Fi networks.

DISCONNECT A NETWORK

Press the side button to access the Control Center.

Press and hold the Wi-Fi button, then select the network you're currently connected to.

Choose the "Forget this network" option.

If you want to reconnect to this network in the future, you will need to re-enter your password (if necessary).

For more details, see the Apple Support article How to connect your Apple Watch to Wi-Fi.

BROWSE THE COLLECTION OF WATCH FACES AVAILABLE ON APPLE WATCH ULTRA

The Watch app's watch face gallery provides a convenient way to browse and select from available watch faces. Once you've found a watch face you like, you can customize it, select complications, and add it to your collection right from the gallery.

ACCESS THE WATCH FACE GALLERY

Launch the Watch app on your iPhone, then select "Watch Face Gallery" located at the bottom.

Select items for a watch face.

In the watch face gallery, select a watch face, then choose a function, such as color or style. As you explore the different options, the preview at the top of the screen updates to reflect your selections, allowing you to preview what it will look like.

EMBED APPLICATIONS IN THE WATCH FACE

Within the watch face gallery, select a watch face and choose a location for the complication, such as "Top Left," "Top Right," or "Bottom." Scroll through the list of available complications for that location and tap the one you prefer. If you don't want complications in that location, swipe up and select "No."

ACCESS YOUR COLLECTION OF WATCH FACES

You can easily see all the watch faces in one place.
1. Open the Watch app on your iPhone.
2. Tap My Watch, then scroll through your collection under My Watch Faces.
3. To change the order of your collection, tap "Edit" in My Watch Faces, then use the Reorder icon next to a watch face to move it up or down.

You can also rearrange the order of your collection directly on your Apple Watch Ultra. While viewing a watch face, press and hold the screen, press and hold again, then drag to move the watch face left or right.

REMOVE A WATCH FACE FROM YOUR COLLECTION

To delete a watch face from the collection, follow these steps:
1. Firmly press the screen on the face of the current watch.
2. Scroll to the watch face you want to delete, swipe up, and tap the "Remove" option.

Alternatively, on your iPhone, you can perform the following steps:
1. Open the Watch app.
2. Tocca "Apple Watch".
3. Go to the "My Watch Faces" section and tap "Edit."
4. Next to the watch faces you want to delete, tap the "Delete" button, then confirm by tapping "Remove."

Keep in mind that you can always add the watch face to your collection if you change your mind.

SHARE APPLE WATCH ULTRA WATCH FACES WITH OTHERS

You have the option to share watch faces with your friends. Shared watch faces can include both watchOS built-in complications and complications created by third-party developers.

Note that the recipient of the watch face must have an Apple Watch with watchOS 7 or later to receive and use the shared watch face.

HOW TO SHARE A WATCH FACE

To share a watch face on your Apple Watch, follow these steps:
1. Go to the watch face you want to share.
2. Press and hold the screen, then tap the "Share" button.
3. Choose the name of the watch face, then tap Don't Include for any watch faces you don't want to share.
4. Select a recipient or tap "Messages" or "Mail."
5. If you opt for "Messages" or "Mail," you can add a contact, a subject (for Mail), and a message.
6. Finally, tap "Send" to share the watch face.

RECEIVE A WATCH FACE

You can accept shared watch faces through Messages, Mail, or by clicking an online link.
1. Open a message, email, or link that contains the shared watch face.
2. Tap the shared clock face.
3. Choose "Add" to include it in your watch faces.

If the shared watch face includes a complication from a third-party app, you can tap the price of the app or the "Get" option to download the app from the App Store. Alternatively, you can select "Continue without this app" to get the watch face without the third-party complication.

APPLE WATCH FACES AND THEIR FEATURES

Apple Watch offers a range of customizable watch faces. Please note that watch face availability may vary depending on location and model. To make sure you have access to the latest watch faces, make sure your software is up-to-date by checking for software updates.

-Watch face with digital activity face

Digital Activity Dial is a dial that prominently presents the time in digital format, accompanied by activity progress, using large, elegant fonts.

-Artist

The "Artist" watch face offers dynamic visuals that change with every touch, offering a wide range of creative combinations, with millions of possibilities.

-Astronomia

The Earth, Moon, and Solar System quadrant features a constantly updated 3D model of the Earth, Moon, or the entire solar system. You can interact with it by tapping the watch face and using the Digital Crown to explore different times, observe the phases of the moon, or explore the positions of planets in the solar system.

-Respiration

This quadrant stimulates relaxation and mindful breathing. Tap to get started.
Customization Options: Style (Classic, Calm, Impact)

-California
The dial of the watch combines Roman and Arabic numerals in its design.

-Chronograph
The watch face features precise time measurement in increments, similar to a traditional analog chronograph. It also includes a stopwatch that can be started directly from the watch face.

-Chronograph Pro
To activate the chronograph function, simply tap the outer edge surrounding the main 12-hour display on this dial. This feature allows you to record time intervals in increments of 60, 30, 6, and 3 seconds.

-Color
This dial shows the time and all functions set in your preferred color.

-Outline (available only on Apple Watch Series 7, Apple Watch Series 8, and Apple Watch Series 9)
This dial slowly switches to displaying the current time. The numbers use a specially designed font that curves around the edges of the screen, smoothly transitioning from hour to hour. To view the numbers as they change from hour to hour, simply tap the watch face and turn the Digital Crown.

-Contour
This watch face is designed to track elapsed time.

-Recognition
The Explore watch face (accessible on Apple Watch with cellular capability) shows green dots that represent cellular signal strength.

-Flame & Liquid

This watch face activates whenever you raise your wrist or interact with the screen.

-GMT

This watch face offers two display options: a 12-hour format to show local time, and a 24-hour format that allows you to display a second time zone.

-Gradient

This dial displays varying color gradients that change over time.

-Infographic
This dial features up to eight richly detailed and colorful complications and sub-dials.

-Kaleidoscope
Choose a photo to generate a watch face with dynamic patterns in different shapes and colors. To change the pattern, tap the watch face, then turn the Digital Crown.

-Metallic Liquid
This watch face activates whenever you lift your wrist or interact with the screen.

-Lunar
This dial illustrates the correlation between the date, time, and moon phases. Simply tap the watch face, then use the Digital Crown to adjust the time to view past or future moon phases.

-Memoji
This watch face shows the Memoji you've created, including all of their different variations.

-Meridiana
This full-screen watch face offers a classic look, complete with four sub-watch faces.

-Metropolitan
This classic, typography-influenced dial features specially crafted numerals that adjust in style and weight when interacted with by tapping the dial or using the Digital Crown. When the wrist is lowered, the numbers turn into pill-like shapes.

-Mickey and Minnie Mouse

Mickey or Minnie can add a playful element to the watch face as their arms move to show the hours and minutes, and their feet mark the seconds.

-Modulate
This dial features six complications presented in a clear and legible typographic layout.

-Compact modular
You have the flexibility to select up to three complications and decide between an analog or digital display with this watch face.

-Modulare Duo (solo Apple Watch Series 7, Apple Watch Series 8 e Apple Watch Series 9)
This dial displays digital time along with the ability to include up to three complications. Notably, two of these complications are presented in sizable rectangular areas, offering a closer look at the specific details of the complications you find most relevant.

-Animation
This watch face features a lovely, animated theme.

-Nike wallpapers, created in collaboration with Nike:
NIKE COMPACT, NIKE REBOUND, NIKE DIGITAL, NIKE ANALOG, NIKE GLOBE, NIKE HYBRID

-Figures
This dial displays the time using analog hands placed on a prominent numerical representation of the time. You have the option to choose from seven distinct styles and a multitude of colors to create the perfect combination.
Figures include monochrome digits and two-colo-r digits.

-Color Schemes
The palette uses dynamic colors to accentuate the various components of the watch face. The slopes align with the hands of the watch and move when the second hand completes a full rotation.

-Viewing photos
With this watch face, a new image greets you every time you lift your wrist or interact with the screen. Select an album, memorable collection, or include up to 24 custom photos.

-Interactive Art
Experience a unique and dynamic masterpiece on your Apple Watch with this watch face. As you rotate the Digital Crown, watch the background transform and interact with the characters as they respond to your tap on the watch face.

-Portrait Photography
The Portraits watch face uses images from your iPhone's photo library, enhancing them with layered effects. It is suitable for photos with people, dogs, cats, landscapes, and more. You can customize it by choosing from

three distinct typography styles and curating up to 24 photos. Every time you raise your wrist or interact with the screen, a new photo will grace the watch face.

-Rainbow-inspired analog
The face of the Analog Pride watch is inspired by the rainbow flag, and its colorful stripes dynamically change when you interact with the watch face.

-Pride Festival
The colors of the Pride flag are displayed on a single dial, available in three distinct styles. Interact with the dial to bring the vibrant pattern to life.

-Digital Pride
Drawing inspiration from the rainbow flag, this watch face features dynamic, moving colored stripes when you interact with the watch face.

-Braid of Pride

Taking inspiration from the rainbow flag, this watch face features vibrant color stripes that sparkle and sparkle when you interact with the watch face.

-Pride Plot

Drawing inspiration from the rainbow flag, this dial features dynamic-colored stripes that respond to touch and shift as you rotate the Digital Crown.

-Minimalist

This sleek watch face embraces simplicity, allowing you to customize your favorite details and features, which are displayed neatly in the corners of the screen.

-Siri

This dial offers precise and valuable information immediately. Conveniently present details such as your next appointment, current traffic conditions for your commute home, or sunset time. A simple tap reveals more information, and you can navigate through your day by turning the Digital Crown. Pressing the Digital Crown returns you to the watch face.

-Curious
This watch face, depicted by the beloved beagle Snoopy, captures the playful essence of the Peanuts dog on your Apple Watch. Snoopy tries his hand at Woodstock and the hands of the clock, adding a delightful touch to your timekeeping. You can opt for the "Sunday Surprise" color scheme, and on Sunday, the background transforms into an homage to the iconic Sunday comic.

-Solar Analog
The "Solar Analog" dial features dynamic lights and shadows that evolve throughout the day, mirroring the sun's journey.

-Sun and Moon
This dial shows a circular 24-hour dial that tracks the movement of the sun, along with an analog or digital dial that moves in the opposite direction.
Tip: To see the whole day, tap the watch face, then use the Digital Crown to check the sunrise and sunset times.

-Path of the Sun
The "Sun Path" watch face shows the position of the Sun in the sky, along with day, date, and time information based on your location and time of day.
Tip: To see the whole day, tap the watch face, then use the Digital Crown to check the sunrise and sunset times.

-Stripe pattern
This watch face allows you to customize the number of stripes, select colors, and adjust the angle to create your own unique pattern.

-Time Frame
This watch face shows a timelapse video with your natural landscape or the urban setting of your choice.

-Toystory

Your beloved Toy Story characters come to life every time you raise your wrist.

-Typographic

The Typographic watch face features three unique custom fonts.

-Unity

The face of the Union watch is inspired by the colors of the Pan-African flag, and its shape dynamically changes as you move, resulting in a distinctive and unique look.

-Unity Lights
This quadrant draws inspiration from Afrofuturism, a philosophy that explores the experiences of the African diaspora through the lenses of science, technology, and self-empowerment.

-Mosaic of Units
Drawing inspiration from the artistic process of creating mosaics, this quadrant represents the resilience and unity of Black communities. It symbolizes the strength that emerges when people are together.

-Functional
This watch face has been designed with convenience and functionality in mind. You have the option to incorporate up to three complications, ensuring that essential information is easily accessible.

-Steam
This watch face comes to life every time you raise your wrist or interact with the screen.

-World Time

This watch face allows you to monitor the time in 24 time zones at the same time. The outer dial positions correspond to various time zones, while the inner dial displays the current time for each location. Touching the globe centers it in the current time zone, indicated by the arrow at 6 o'clock.

The sun and moon icons indicate sunrise and sunset at your location, while the light and dark regions on the globe represent the progression of day and night on Earth.

-Very large

Choose this option when you need the most available screen space. Adding a complication will take up the entire screen in this mode.

PAIR APPLE WATCH ULTRA WITH BLUETOOTH AUDIO DEVICES

Stream audio from Apple Watch Ultra to Bluetooth headphones or speakers, even when your iPhone isn't nearby.

Tip: If you've already paired AirPods with your iPhone, you can use them with Apple Watch Ultra without any additional setup; Simply start playing the audio.

PAIR BLUETOOTH AUDIO DEVICES

To hear most audio on Apple Watch Ultra, including Siri, phone calls, voicemails, and voice memos (note that these use the watch's speaker for playback), you'll need Bluetooth headphones or speakers. Here's how to set them up:

1. Make sure your Bluetooth headphones or speakers are in "discoverable" mode by following the device's instructions.
2. Open the Settings app on your Apple Watch Ultra and tap Bluetooth.
3. Look for your device in the list and tap on it to pair it.

Alternatively, you can access Bluetooth settings by tapping the AirPlay button on the playback screen of the Audiobooks, Music, Now Playing, and Podcasts apps.

SELECT AN AUDIO OUTPUT SOURCE.

To select your preferred audio output device, simply press the side button to enter the Control Center, then tap the Audio Output icon. From there, you can choose the specific device you want to use for audio playback. Also, for essential hearing safety information, see the "Important safety information for Apple Watch Ultra" document.

MANAGE YOUR APPLE WATCH FROM YOUR IPHONE

For people with physical and mobility issues, it may be more convenient to control their Apple Watch via the larger display of the paired iPhone. Using the Apple Watch Screen Mirroring feature, you can use your Apple Watch using iPhone accessibility features like Voice Control and Switch Control. This method allows you to use various input methods, including voice commands, sound gestures, head tracking, or third-party switches designed specifically for iPhones, instead of interacting directly with the Apple Watch screen.

The Apple Watch mirroring feature is supported on Apple Watch Series 6, Apple Watch Series 7, Apple Watch Series 8, and Apple Watch Series 9.

Here's how to enable it:

1. Open the Settings app on the paired iPhone.
2. Go to Accessibility > Mirroring Apple Watch, then turn on Mirror Apple Watch.

Once activated, the Apple Watch screen will be mirrored to your iPhone. You can perform the following actions using gestures on the duplicate image:

*   Swipe: Swipe up or down.
*   Navigate between screens: Swipe left or right.
*   Access the Digital Crown features: Tap the Digital Crown.
*   Use the side button: Tap the side button that appears on the screen.
*   Activate Siri: Press and hold the Digital Crown on the screen to activate Siri.

END A PAIRING AND RESET YOUR APPLE WATCH

There are two methods to erase data and reset Apple Watch settings:

1. Erase Apple Watch from iPhone**:** This action erases the content and deletes the activation lock, making it suitable for resale or gift to another user.

2. Erase Apple Watch: This action erases all data and settings on the Apple Watch but does not unpair it from your iPhone. It's useful when you intend to keep your Apple Watch but want to start over.

UNPAIR YOUR APPLE WATCH AND REMOVE ACTIVATION LOCK:
- Open the Watch app on your iPhone.
- Tap "My Watch" and select "All Apple Watches."
- Locate your Apple Watch, tap the About button next to it, then tap Unpair Apple Watch.

As a result, your Apple Watch will be erased and unlinked from your iCloud account, the activation lock will be removed, and you can proceed to reconfigure the device. For more information, see the Apple Support article titled "About Activation Lock for Apple Watch."

ERASE YOUR APPLE WATCH WITHOUT UNPAIRING IT
- Open the Settings app on your Apple Watch.
- Go to "General" > "Reset", tap "Erase All Content and Settings" and enter the passcode if prompted.
- If you have an Apple Watch (cellular), decide whether to keep or remove your cellular plan:
  - Keep the plan if you plan to pair your Apple Watch with your iPhone again.
  - Remove your plan if you want to pair your Apple Watch with another iPhone, or if you want to cancel your cellular plan subscription (contact your carrier to cancel your subscription).
  - Once you've completed these steps, proceed to set up your Apple Watch again, and when prompted, restore from a backup.

Alternatively, you can perform this action through the Watch app on your iPhone. Just tap on "Apple Watch", go to "General" > "Erase" and select "Erase Apple Watch All Content and Settings".

To remove your cellular plan: If you have an Apple Watch with cellular service and want to remove your cellular plan, follow these steps:
- Open the Watch app on your iPhone.
- Tap My Watch, then tap Cellular.
- Locate your cellular plan and tap the About button next to it.
- Choose "Delete [carrier name] plan" and confirm your decision.

In some cases, you may need to contact your carrier to remove your Apple Watch from your cellular plan.

In case you forget your Apple Watch passcode

In case your Apple Watch gets disabled due to forgotten passcode attempts or too many incorrect entries, you have the option to erase it directly from your Apple Watch or through your paired iPhone and later set it up again. Here's how:

Important note: If Erase Data is enabled, your Apple Watch data will be erased after 10 unsuccessful passcode attempts.

ERASING APPLE WATCH:
1. Make sure your Apple Watch is charged, then press and hold the side button until you see the slider options.
2. Continue to hold the side button and hold the Digital Crown at the same time. This action will display the "Erase All Content and Settings" screen.
3. Tap "Clear" and then confirm your selection by tapping "Erase" once more.
4. After that, proceed to set up your Apple Watch again. When prompted, you can choose to restore from a backup.

ERASE YOUR APPLE WATCH USING YOUR PAIRED IPHONE:
1. Open the Watch app on your iPhone and select "Apple Watch."
2. Tap "General," scroll down, then choose "Erase."
3. Tap Erase Apple Watch All Content and Settings, then confirm your decision by selecting Erase All Content and Settings.

If your Apple Watch has Cell capabilities, you'll need to decide whether to keep or remove your cellular plan:

- Keep the plan if you intend to pair your Apple Watch with your iPhone again.
- Remove your plan if you plan to pair your Apple Watch with another iPhone, or if you're thinking about canceling your cellular plan subscription (contact your carrier to cancel your subscription).

After the erasing process, proceed to set up your Apple Watch again, and when prompted, you can choose to restore from a backup.

Keep in mind that even after you erase your Apple Watch, Activation Lock remains on. Activation Lock requires your Apple ID and password to perform the following actions:
- Unpair your Apple Watch and iPhone.
- Pair and use Apple Watch with a new iPhone.
- Turn off Find My on your device.

RESTORE YOUR APPLE WATCH FROM A BACKUP

Apple Watch comes with an auto-backup feature that conveniently backs up your watch data to your iPhone. This allows for easy recovery using a previously stored backup. These Apple Watch backups are included in your iPhone backups, regardless of whether they're stored in iCloud, on your Mac, or on your PC. It's important to note that if your backups are stored in iCloud, you won't have direct access to view their contents.

1. BACK UP YOUR APPLE WATCH:
- When you pair your Apple Watch with your iPhone for the first time, your watch data is continuously and automatically backed up to your iPhone.
- In case you decide to unpair your devices, a backup of your Apple Watch is created first.

For more details and guidance on backing up your Apple Watch, you can refer to the Apple Support article titled "Backing up your Apple Watch."

2. INTRODUCTION RESTORING APPLE WATCH FROM A BACKUP:
- If you intend to pair your Apple Watch with the same iPhone again or buy a new Apple Watch, you can choose to restore your watch from a backup.
- Simply select "Restore from Backup" and choose a backup stored on your iPhone.

It's worth mentioning that when an Apple Watch is managed for a family member, it automatically backs up to that family member's iCloud account whenever it's connected to power and a Wi-Fi network. If you want to disable iCloud backups for that specific Apple Watch, you can do so by going to the Settings app on the managed Apple Watch, then navigating to "[account name] > iCloud > iCloud backup" and afterward turning off the iCloud Backup option.

Updating your Apple Watch software.

CHECKING AND INSTALLING SOFTWARE UPDATES:
1. Launch the Watch app on your iPhone.
2. Go to "Apple Watch" and then proceed to "General" > "Software Update".
3. If an update is accessible, you can select "Download and Install."

You also have the option to check for updates directly on your Apple Watch by following these steps:
- Go to the Settings app on your Apple Watch.
- Go to "General" > "Software Update".

For more complete information about updating your Apple Watch software, you can refer to the Apple Support article titled "Updating your Apple Watch."

UPDATING YOUR APPLE WATCH SOFTWARE

To make sure your Apple Watch is running with the latest software improvements, you can initiate an update by checking for available updates through the Watch app on your iPhone. Follow these steps:

Checking and Installing Software Updates:
1. Launch the Watch app on your iPhone.

2. Go to "Apple Watch" and then proceed to "General" > "Software Update".
3. If an update is accessible, you can select "Download and Install."

You also have the option to check for updates directly on your Apple Watch by following these steps:

- Go to the Settings app on your Apple Watch.
- Go to "General" > "Software Update".

APP ICON	APP NAME
	ACTIVITY
	ALARM CLOCK
	APP STORE
	AUDIOLIBRI
	O2 LEVELS
	CALCULATOR
	CALENDAR
	CAMERA
	COMPASS
	CONTACTS
	CYCLE TRACKING
	ECG
	FIND DEVICES
	OBJECT SEARCH
	FINDING PEOPLE
	HEARTBEAT
	HOUSE
	MAIL
	MAPS
	DRUGS
	MEMOJI
	MESSAGES
	MUSIC
	CALLS
	PHOTO
	MEMORANDUM
	REMOTE
	SETTINGS
	SHORTCUTS
	WEATHER FORECAST
	FORMATION

OPEN APPS ON APPLE WATCH ULTRA

The Home screen gives you access to all the apps on your Apple Watch Ultra, allowing you to open them with ease. Additionally, the app list gives you quick access to recently used apps, making it convenient to switch between them.

VIEW APPS IN GRID OR LIST FORMAT

You have the option to view apps in grid or list format on the home screen. When you set up your Apple Watch for the first time, choose the view you want. If you want to change it later, follow these steps:

1. Press the Digital Crown from the watch face to access the home screen.
2. Scroll down to the bottom of the screen using the Digital Crown.
3. Select Grid View or List View.

Alternatively, you can go to the Settings app, tap "App View," and then choose between "Grid View" or "List View."

ACCESS APPS FROM THE HOME SCREEN

The method to open apps depends on the view you choose.

In grid view: Just tap the app icon. To see more apps, turn the Digital Crown.

List view: Scroll through the list by turning the Digital Crown, then tap the app you want to open.

To return to the home screen from an open app, press the Digital Crown once, then press it again to switch to the watch face.

USE THE ACTION BUTTON ON APPLE WATCH ULTRA.

The Action button acts as a convenient physical control to access various functions. For example, pressing the Action button located on the left side of Apple Watch Ultra can open apps and activate personalized features based on your favorite activity. You can also assign a Siri shortcut to the Action button.
Here's how to set it up:

1. Open the Settings app on your Apple Watch Ultra.
2. Tap the Action button, then select an action, such as Workout, Rebuild, or Dive.
3. Tap the back button to explore other options, if available.

For example, if you choose Workout, you can tap the back button to return to the action list, then select "First Press" to specify a particular workout to start when you press the Action key.

In some cases, some apps can perform specific actions when you press the Action button and the side button at the same time. For example, if you've configured the Action button to start the stopwatch, pressing both buttons together will pause it.

ACCESS AN APP FROM THE LIST OF APPS

To open an app from the list of recently used applications, follow these steps:

1. Double press the Digital Crown on your Apple Watch Ultra.
2. Turn the Digital Crown to scroll through the list of apps you've recently used.

Keep in mind that apps in active sessions, such as Maps navigation or workouts, will appear at the top of the list.

3. Tap on the app you want to open, and it will launch.

DELETE AN APP FROM THE LIST OF APPS

To remove an app from the list of recently used applications, follow these steps:

1. Double-click the Digital Crown on your Apple Watch Ultra.
2. Turn the Digital Crown until you find the app you want to delete.
3. Swipe left on the app icon.
4. Finally, tap on the "Delete" option to remove the app from the list.

REARRANGE APPS ON APPLE WATCH ULTRA
REORDER APPS IN GRID VIEW ON APPLE WATCH ULTRA
1. On your Apple Watch Ultra, access the home screen by pressing the Digital Crown.
2. If you're currently in List view, go to the bottom of the screen and select Grid View. Alternatively, you can open the Settings app on your Apple Watch Ultra, go to "App View," and choose "Grid View."
3. To reorder an app, touch and hold it, then drag it to the desired location.
4. Once you're done rearranging your apps, simply press the Digital Crown to exit this mode.

Alternatively, you can rearrange your apps as follows:
1. Open the Watch app on your paired iPhone.
2. Tap My Watch, then select App View.
3. Choose "Arrangement."
4. Touch and hold an app icon, then drag it to the desired location.

Note that in the list view, apps are automatically arranged alphabetically.

TO UNINSTALL AN APP FROM YOUR APPLE WATCH ULTRA, FOLLOW THESE STEPS
1. Press and hold the app icon on the home screen.
2. Tap the "X" that appears to remove the app from your Apple Watch Ultra. Keep in mind that the app will still be kept on your paired iPhone unless you delete it from there as well.

In the list view:
1. Swipe left on the app.
2. Tap the Trash icon to remove it from your Apple Watch Ultra.

Keep in mind that if you remove an app from your iPhone, it will also be deleted from your Apple Watch Ultra. If necessary, you can reinstall it from the App Store on your iPhone or Apple Watch Ultra. Keep in mind that not all apps can be removed from your Apple Watch Ultra.

TO ADJUST AN APP'S SETTINGS ON APPLE WATCH ULTRA, FOLLOW THESE STEPS
1. Open the Watch app on your paired iPhone.
2. Tap "My Watch" to access your device's settings.
3. Scroll down to see the list of apps installed on your Apple Watch Ultra.
4. Tap the specific app for which you want to change the settings.

You can also keep in mind that some restrictions you set up on your iPhone within the "Settings" app under "Screen Time" > "Content & Privacy" may also apply to your Apple Watch Ultra. For example, if you disable the Camera app on your iPhone, the camera icon will be removed from the home screen of your Apple Watch Ultra.

TO CHECK THE STORAGE ALLOCATION FOR APPS ON APPLE WATCH ULTRA, FOLLOW THESE STEPS

1. Go to the "Settings" app on your Apple Watch Ultra.
2. Go to "General" and select "Space."

Alternatively, you can perform the same action using your paired iPhone:
1. Launch the "Watch" app on your iPhone.
2. Tocca "Apple Watch".
3. Go to "General" and then select "Storage."

These steps will allow you to view information about the total storage used, available storage, and individual storage consumption of each app on your Apple Watch Ultra.

EXPAND COLLECTION APPS ON APPLE WATCH ULTRA
Apple Watch Ultra offers a selection of built-in apps, catering to various communication, health, fitness, and timing needs. Plus, you have the flexibility to install third-party apps through your iPhone, get new apps from the App Store directly on your Apple Watch Ultra, or through your iPhone. These apps are neatly organized on a single Home screen for easy access.

Note that you can enable automatic download of iOS versions of apps you've added to your Apple Watch Ultra. To do this, go to Settings on your Apple Watch Ultra, tap "App Store" and turn on "Automatic Downloads". Making sure this feature is turned on allows you to keep your Apple Watch Ultra apps up to date with the latest versions.

TO ADD APPS FROM THE APP STORE TO APPLE WATCH ULTRA
1. Launch the App Store on your Apple Watch Ultra.
2. Use the Digital Crown to scroll through featured apps and app collections.
3. If you find a collection you're interested in, tap it to see other apps within that category.
4. To download a free app, simply tap the "Get" button. If you want to buy an app, tap the price displayed.
5. If you see the "Download" button instead of a price, it means that you have already purchased the app and can reinstall it at no additional cost. Please note that for some apps, you may need to install the corresponding iOS version on your iPhone.
6. To locate a particular app, tap the Search icon located at the top left of the screen. You can then enter the name of the app using text input, voice dictation, or the handwriting option. Alternatively, you can select a category to explore trending app categories.
7. If you want to use the handwriting feature, swipe up from the bottom of the screen and select the appropriate option.

Keep in mind that when you use Apple Watch Ultra with cellular service, data charges may apply, and the availability of the handwriting feature may vary depending on your language settings.

TO SELECTIVELY INSTALL APPS FROM YOUR IPHONE TO YOUR APPLE WATCH ULTRA

1. Open the Watch app on your iPhone.
2. Tocca "Apple Watch".
3. Tap "General."
4. Turn off "Automatic App Installation."
5. Scroll down to the "Available Apps" section.
6. Locate the apps you want to install and tap "Install" next to each one.

By disabling the "Automatic App Install" option, you get more control over which apps are installed on your Apple Watch Ultra, allowing you to choose only the ones you prefer.

MANAGE AND RESPOND TO NOTIFICATIONS ON YOUR APPLE WATCH ULTRA.
Apps can send notifications to Apple Watch Ultra, including event invitations, messages, noise alerts, and activity reminders. These notifications can be viewed in real-time or saved for later viewing. Refer to the important safety information to avoid distractions in the Apple Watch Ultra guidelines.

TAKE IMMEDIATE ACTION WHEN YOU RECEIVE A NOTIFICATION.
When a notification arrives, simply raise your wrist to see it. The appearance of the notification varies depending on whether the screen is active or not.
- Active screen: A compact banner appears at the top of the screen.
- Screen off: A full-screen notification appears.

To read the notification, tap it. To close it, scroll down or scroll to the bottom and tap Close.

CHECK UNREAD NOTIFICATIONS ON APPLE WATCH ULTRA
Check unread notifications on Apple Watch Ultra:
1. Swipe down from the top of the screen or turn the Digital Crown to open Notification Center.

Note: You can't open Notification Center from the Home screen. Press the Digital Crown to access the watch face first, or open an app, then open Notification Center.
2. Scroll through the list of notifications by swiping up or down.
3. Tap a notification to read or reply to it.

Siri can also read notifications aloud through the Apple Watch speaker or connected Bluetooth headphones by saying "Read me notifications."
To clear a notification without reading it, swipe left and tap X. To clear all notifications, firmly press the top of the screen and tap Clear All.
If you're using group notifications, tap a group to open it, then tap a notification.
To avoid the red indicator on your watch face, go to the Settings app on your Apple Watch Ultra, tap Notifications, and turn off Notification Indicator.

TURN OFF ALL NOTIFICATIONS ON APPLE WATCH ULTRA
To turn off both sounds and haptic feedback for notifications on Apple Watch Ultra, you can use Do Not Disturb:
1. Press the side button to access the Control Center.
2. Tap the Silent button to mute sounds, but keep the haptic feedback.
3. If you want to disable both sounds and haptic feedback, follow these steps:
a. Press the side button to open Control Center.
b. Tap the Do Not Disturb button or turn on the Focus.
c. Choose an option: "On", "On for 1 hour" or "On until tonight/On until tomorrow morning".
Tip: You can quickly mute your Apple Watch Ultra by covering the watch screen with the palm of your hand for at least three seconds. Make sure the "Cover to Mute" option is turned on in the Settings app under Sounds & Haptics to use this feature.

CHANGE NOTIFICATION PREFERENCES ON APPLE WATCH ULTRA
By default, the notification settings for apps on Apple Watch Ultra mirror those set up on iPhone. However, you have the flexibility to customize how specific apps display notifications to you.

CUSTOMIZE THE APPP'S NOTIFICATION PREFERENCES
In the Watch app on iPhone:
1. Go to Notifications > your Apple Watch.
2. Select the desired app (e.g., Messages).
3. Tap Customize, then choose one of the following:
   - Allow notifications: View notifications in Notification Center.
   - Send to Notification Center: Send notifications directly to Notification Center without sound or display.
   - Disabled notifications: Disables notifications for the app.
     You can also customize how notifications are grouped:
   - No: No grouping.
   - Automatically: Grouped based on information provided by the app (e.g., news notifications by channel).
   - By app: All app notifications are grouped together.

Tip: Some apps allow you to customize notification types, such as Calendar, which allows you to receive notifications only for specific calendars or actions, and Mail, which allows you to select email accounts for notifications.

CUSTOMIZE NOTIFICATIONS DIRECTLY ON APPLE WATCH ULTRA

To manage notification preferences on your Apple Watch Ultra, swipe left on a notification and tap the More button. Options may include:

- Turn off alerts for one hour or No alerts today: Notifications are sent to Notification Center with no sound or display for a specified period of time. To turn alerts back on, tap Turn on alerts.
- Add to summary: Future notifications from apps appear in the summary on iPhone.
- Turn off urgent notifications: Prevents urgent notifications from being sent immediately.
- Off: Disables notifications from the app; turn them back on in the Watch app on your iPhone.

DISPLAY NOTIFICATIONS ON THE LOCK SCREEN

You can customize how notifications appear on the lock screen of your Apple Watch Ultra.

Open the Settings app on your Apple Watch Ultra.

Tap Notifications.

Select one of the following options:

1. Show summary when locked: This option displays a summary of notifications when the watch is locked, including the name, icon, and a short title of the app.
2. Tap to show the full notification: When you raise your wrist to check a notification, you'll initially see a short summary, followed by the full details after a few seconds. For example, with a message notification, you'll see the sender's name first and then the message itself. Enabling this option ensures that the full notification appears only when you tap it.
3. Show notifications with your wrist down: By default, notifications don't appear on your Apple Watch Ultra when your wrist is down. Enabling this option allows notifications to appear even when the watch is facing away from you.

ENTERING PHONE NUMBERS

If you need to manually enter a phone number during a call, follow these steps:
1. Open the Phone app: Launch the Phone app on your Apple Watch.
2. Start a FaceTime audio call: Start a FaceTime audio call.
3. Access the keyboard: Tap the More Options button, then select Keyboard. You can use this keypad to enter additional numbers during the call.

ANSWER CALLS WITH YOUR APPLE WATCH

RECEIVING A CALL

When you receive a call or call notification, you can easily manage it using your Apple Watch:
1. Call Notification: When you hear or feel a call notification, raise your wrist to check who is calling you.
2. Send to voicemail: to send a call directly to voicemail, tap the "Reject" button on the incoming call notification.
3. Reply on Apple Watch: If you want to reply using your Apple Watch, tap the Reply button. You can speak through the watch's built-in microphone and speaker, or through a paired Bluetooth device.
4. Reply with iPhone or text: Tap the More Options button, then select an option. If you choose "Answer on iPhone", the call will be put on hold and the caller will hear a repeated tone until you answer on your iPhone. If you can't locate your iPhone, tap Play iPhone on your Apple Watch to help you find it.

DURING A CALL

During a call, you have several options to manage it effectively:
1. Transfer call to iPhone: If you're making a call using your Apple Watch and want to transfer it to your iPhone, unlock your iPhone and tap the green button or bar at the top of the screen.
2. Mute a call: You can quickly mute an incoming call by placing the palm of your hand on the screen for three seconds. Make sure the "Cover to Mute" option is enabled by going to the Settings app on your Apple Watch, tapping "Sounds & Haptics," and turning on "Cover to Mute."
3. Adjusting the call volume: To adjust the volume of your calls, simply turn the Digital Crown. You can also mute your microphone during a call by tapping the "Mute" button, which is useful during audio conferences or when you need to mute yourself.
4. Dialing additional numbers: If you need to enter additional numbers during a call (for example, for automated systems), tap the "More Options" button, then select "Keypad." This allows you to enter the necessary numbers using the numeric keypad.
5. Transfer to other audio devices: In case you have multiple audio devices, you can choose to transfer the call to another device by tapping on the "More Options" button and selecting the desired device.

MAKE CALLS WITH YOUR APPLE WATCH
START CALLS WITH YOUR VOICE:
Siri makes it easy to start calls on your Apple Watch using your voice. You can say commands like:
- "Call Mark."
- "Call 555 555 2949."
- "Call Mario with FaceTime audio."

MAKE A CALL: TO MANUALLY MAKE A CALL USING APPLE WATCH:
1. Open the Phone app: Launch the Phone app on your Apple Watch.
2. Access your contacts: Tap Contacts and use the Digital Crown to scroll through your contacts.
3. Select Contact: Tap the contact you want to call, then tap the Phone button.
4. Choose Call Type: You can start a regular phone call by tapping the phone number or start a FaceTime audio call by tapping FaceTime Audio.
5. Adjust the call volume: During the call, you can easily adjust the volume by turning the Digital Crown.

Tip: If you want to call someone you've recently spoken to, tap Recents and select a contact. To call a favorite contact from your iPhone's Phone app, tap "Favorites" and choose a contact.

GROUP FACETIME CALLS:
With watchOS 10 and later, you can also make Group FaceTime calls directly from your Apple Watch:
1. Open the Phone app: Launch the Phone app on your Apple Watch.
2. Start a FaceTime audio call: Start a FaceTime audio call with a contact.
3. Add participants: To invite more people to the call, you can do one of the following:
   - Tap the "More Options" button, select "Add People," and choose a contact.
   - If someone else has already joined the call, tap "2 people," then tap the "Add" button and select another contact.

MAKE CALLS OVER WI-FI
If your carrier supports Wi-Fi calling, your Apple Watch can make and receive calls over Wi-Fi, even without your paired iPhone nearby. To use this feature:
1. Check carrier support: Make sure your carrier supports Wi-Fi calling. You can check this by referring to the Apple Support article on Wi-Fi calling and enabling it on your iPhone.
2. Enable Wi-Fi calling on iPhone: On your iPhone, go to Settings > phone, tap "Wi-Fi Calling" and enable "Wi-Fi Calling on this iPhone" and "Wi-Fi Calling for Other Devices".
3. Start a Wi-Fi call: On your Apple Watch, open the Phone app, select a contact, and tap the Call button. You can then choose a phone number or FaceTime address to make the call.

Note: While you can make emergency calls over Wi-Fi, it's a good idea to use your iPhone over a cellular network to get more accurate location information.

USE APPLE WATCH ULTRA REGARDLESS OF HOW CLOSE YOUR IPHONE IS

With Apple Watch Ultra cellular service and an active plan, you can stay connected even when your iPhone isn't nearby. Here's what you can do:

- Listen to music, podcasts, and audiobooks
- Record and play back voice memos
- Use Transportation Cards and Student ID Cards
- Locate people, devices, and objects
- Use the clock, set alarms, timers, and use the stopwatch
- Browse photos from synced albums
- Make purchases with Apple Pay
- View calendar events
- Track physical activity and workouts
- Track various health metrics, including heart rate, sleep, blood oxygen levels, menstrual cycles, and practice mindfulness and relaxation exercises
- Measures ambient sound levels and headphone audio levels

In addition, Apple Watch Ultra comes with a built-in GPS receiver for accurate distance and speed tracking during outdoor workouts without iPhone. It also includes a barometric altimeter for accurate altitude data, with the always-on altimeter to show real-time elevation changes.

WHEN APPLE WATCH ULTRA IS CONNECTED TO A WI-FI NETWORK

When your Apple Watch Ultra is connected to a Wi-Fi network, you can still perform the following tasks (even if your iPhone is turned off):

- Download apps from the App Store
- Send messages
- Make calls (if you've enabled Wi-Fi calling or want to make a FaceTime audio call and you're within range of a Wi-Fi network)
- Use Walkie-Talkie
- Stream music, podcasts, and audiobooks to Apple Watch Ultra
- Add Music
- Check the current weather conditions
- Monitor stock
- Control Smart Home Devices
- Use third-party apps that support Wi-Fi connectivity

Apple Watch Ultra uses Bluetooth® wireless technology to connect to your iPhone and uses the device for various wireless functions. It can independently set up Wi-Fi networks and access established or connected Wi-Fi networks through the paired iPhone device. For details, see the Apple Support article on Bluetooth, Wi-Fi, and cellular on Apple Watch.

USING APPLE WATCH WITH DUAL SIM ON IPHONE
SET UP DUAL SIM WITH APPLE WATCH

If you've set up multiple cellular plans on your iPhone with Dual SIM technology, you can add more lines to your Apple Watch with cellular capability.

Every cellular plan on your iPhone must be supported by a compatible carrier and support Apple Watch with cellular service.

ADDING DATA PLANS FROM MULTIPLE CARRIERS

During the initial setup of your Apple Watch, you can add a data plan. Alternatively, you can add an additional data plan later through the Watch app.

To add a new plan, open the Watch app, tap My Watch, select Cellular, then choose Set Up Cellular or Add New Plan.

MOVING FROM ONE FLOOR TO ANOTHER

You can switch between cellular plans on your Apple Watch by going to cellular settings on the device itself or through the Watch app on your iPhone.

When you switch plans, choose your preferred plan from the ones you've added.

RECEIVE CALLS ON APPLE WATCH WITH MULTIPLE PLANS

When connected to your iPhone, your Apple Watch can receive calls from both lines, displaying the line from which the call originated.

If you answer a call, your Apple Watch will use the line that received the call.

When your iPhone isn't nearby, Apple Watch will receive calls based on the line you select in the Watch app.

RECEIVE MESSAGES ON APPLE WATCH WITH MULTIPLE PLANS

Your Apple Watch can receive messages from both cellular plans when it's connected to your iPhone.

When you reply to a message, your Apple Watch will use the line from which the message was received.

In situations where your iPhone isn't present but your Apple Watch is connected to cellular or Wi-Fi, you can send and receive iMessages.

This setup allows you to use multiple cellular plans on your Apple Watch, ensuring you stay connected seamlessly with the flexibility to choose your preferred line for calls and texts based on your circumstances. Select a photo album and manage storage on Apple Watch

SET UP AND USE CELLULAR SERVICE ON APPLE WATCH ULTRA

With Apple Watch Ultra and a cellular connection on the same carrier as your iPhone, you can make calls, reply to messages, use Walkie-Talkie, stream music and podcasts, receive notifications, and more, even when your iPhone isn't nearby. Please note that cellular network services may not be accessible in all areas or with all carriers.

MOVE AN EXISTING CELLULAR PLAN TO A NEW APPLE WATCH ULTRA

To move your cellular plan from your current Apple Watch to your new Apple Watch Ultra, follow these steps:
1. While wearing your current Apple Watch, open the Watch app on your paired iPhone.
2. Tap My Watch, then select Cellular.
3. Tap the Info button next to your cellular plan.
4. Choose the "Delete [carrier name] plan" option and confirm your decision.
5. You may need to contact your carrier to remove your current Apple Watch from your cellular plan.
6. Remove your current Apple Watch and put on your new Apple Watch Ultra.
7. Tap My Watch, then select Cellular.
8. Follow the instructions provided to activate cellular service on your new watch.
9. You can enable or disable the cellular connection.

Apple Watch Ultra with an active cellular plan will automatically use the best available network connection, which can be iPhone when it's nearby, a previously connected Wi-Fi network, or a cellular connection. However, you can manually turn off the cellular connection, for example, to save battery power. Here are the steps to do so:
1. Press the side button to access Control Center on your Apple Watch Ultra.
2. Tap the Cellular button, then turn Cellular on or off.

When your Apple Watch Ultra has an active cellular connection and you don't have your iPhone nearby, the Cellular button will appear green.

Keep in mind that keeping the cellular network on for long periods can impact battery life, and some apps may not update without a connection to your iPhone. For details, see the Apple Watch Battery Overview website.

USE SIRI ON YOUR APPLE WATCH ULTRA

USEFUL SIRI VOICE COMMANDS

You can use Siri on Apple Watch Ultra to complete various tasks and get answers to your questions directly. For example, you can ask Siri to translate phrases in other languages, identify songs with instant Shazam results, or request information from the web, including a short excerpt from each page. You can then tap "Open Page" to view the page on your Apple Watch Ultra. Siri can simplify tasks that usually involve multiple steps.

Keep in mind that Siri availability may vary by language and region. For more information, you can see the Apple Support article "WatchOS feature availability."

HOW TO USE SIRI

Here's how to interact with Siri on Apple Watch Ultra:
1. Raise your wrist and speak:
   - To activate Siri in this way, just raise your wrist and start talking.
   - You can disable this feature by going to Settings on your Apple Watch Ultra, tapping Siri, and turning off "Raise to Talk."
2. Use the "Hey Siri" command:
   - Just say "Hey Siri" or just "Siri" followed by the question or command.
   - You can turn off this feature by opening the Settings app on your Apple Watch Ultra, tapping Siri, and turning off Siri or Hey Siri.
3. Press and hold the Digital Crown:
   - Press and hold the Digital Crown until the listening indicator appears, then say the command.
   - You can turn off this feature by going to the Settings app on your Apple Watch Ultra, tapping Siri, and disabling "Press Digital Crown."

RECEIVE AND RESPOND TO INCOMING NOTIFICATIONS WITH SIRI USING AIRPODS OR BEATS HEADPHONES ON APPLE WATCH ULTRA

When you're using compatible AirPods or Beats headphones, Siri can read notifications from various apps without the need to unlock your iPhone. Siri remains unobtrusive, listening to your responses after reviewing notifications, eliminating the need to say 'Hey Siri.'"

ENABLE THE "READ NOTIFICATIONS ALOUD" FEATURE

Wear compatible headphones correctly according to their type.

Pair your headphones with your Apple Watch Ultra.

Go to the Settings app on your Apple Watch Ultra.

Go to Siri > Speak Notifications Aloud and enable the Read Notifications Aloud option.

Alternatively, you can open the Settings app on your iPhone, go to Notifications > Read notifications aloud, and turn on Read notifications aloud.

Note: Siri can read unread notifications from Notification Center, using the Apple Watch Ultra speaker or connected Bluetooth headphones. Just say, 'Read me the notifications.'"

<u>**SELECT THE APPS THAT CAN SEND YOU NOTIFICATIONS THROUGH SIRI**</u>

You can specify the apps for which you want notifications to be read aloud.

Make sure you are wearing the appropriate headphones according to their type.

Go to the Settings app on your Apple Watch Ultra.

Go to Siri > Read notifications aloud, scroll through the list, and select the apps you want to enable reading notifications for.

<u>**REPLY TO A MESSAGE**</u>

You can say, "Answer, that's great news."

Siri will repeat your answer and ask you for confirmation before sending it. To send replies without confirmation, you can turn on Reply Without Confirmation by going to the Settings app on your Apple Watch Ultra, signing in to Siri > Read notifications aloud, scrolling to the bottom of the page, and turning it on.

<u>**LET SIRI ANNOUNCE THE CALLER'S NAME ON APPLE WATCH ULTRA**</u>

Siri can speak the caller's name and notifications from apps like Messages on compatible headphone models. The "Read Caller Name" feature also works with supported third-party apps.

Here's how to enable it:
1. Open the Settings app on your Apple Watch Ultra.
2. Tap Siri.
3. Turn on the "Read Caller Name" option.

When you receive a call, the caller's name will be announced, and you can choose to answer it by saying "Yes" or reject the call by saying "No."

SET AN ALARM ON APPLE WATCH

Use the Alarms app to make your Apple Watch sound or vibrate at a specific time.

Siri tip: You can also try saying, "Set a recurring alarm for six in the morning."

<u>**HOW TO SET AN ALARM ON YOUR APPLE WATCH**</u>
1. Open the Alarms app on your Apple Watch.
2. Tap the Add button.
3. Select AM or PM, and then choose the hours and minutes for the alarm.
   Note: This step is not necessary when using the 24-hour format.
4. Use the Digital Crown to adjust the time, then tap the checkmark button.
5. To turn the alarm on or off, tap the alarm switch. You can also tap the alarm time to configure settings like snooze, label, and delay.

Tip: To create a silent alarm that vibrates only on your wrist without making any sound, turn on silent mode.

<u>**SYNC ALARMS BETWEEN IPHONE AND APPLE WATCH**</u>
1. Create the alarm on your iPhone.
2. Launch the Watch app on your iPhone.
3. Select your Apple Watch, then tap Clock.

4. Enable the "Duplicate Alerts from iPhone" option.

With this setting enabled, your Apple Watch will provide notifications for alarms set on your iPhone, allowing you to snooze or dismiss them. Please note that your iPhone will not provide notifications for alarms set on your Apple Watch.

HOW TO USE APPLE WATCH AS A BEDSIDE ALARM CLOCK
1. On your Apple Watch, open the Settings app.
2. Switch to General > Night mode.
3. Enable "Night Mode".

Enabling Night Mode on your connected and charging Apple Watch turns it into a bedside alarm clock. Displays the charging status, current time, date, and all set alarms. Checking the time is as simple as tapping the screen or clock, or gently touching the bedside table. Alarms you've set with the Alarms app will gently wake you up with a unique sound, and you can stop the alarm by pressing the side button, or snooze it for another 9 minutes by tapping the Digital Crown.

HOW TO ADD AUDIOBOOKS TO YOUR APPLE WATCH
1. Open the Watch app on your iPhone.
2. Tocca "Apple Watch".
3. Scroll down and select "Audiobooks."
4. Tap "Add Audiobook" and choose the audiobooks you want to add to your Apple Watch.

Keep in mind that only Apple Books audiobooks can be synced to your Apple Watch. Audiobooks from other sources are not supported. If there is enough storage space available on your Apple Watch, the entire audiobook you are listening to and those listed under "Unread" will be synced automatically. Plus, if space allows, up to five hours of each audiobook you add will be downloaded to your Apple Watch. Note that audiobooks sync to the watch when it's connected to a power source.

HOW TO PLAY AUDIOBOOKS ON YOUR APPLE WATCH
1. Open the Audiobooks app on your Apple Watch.
2. Choose the audiobook you want to listen to from the synced collection.
3. Tap the audiobook to start playing it.

Enjoy your audiobook on your Apple Watch!

In addition, you can also listen to audiobooks that have been purchased by other Family Sharing members from Apple Books. To do this, follow these steps:
1. On the Audiobooks screen, tap "My Family."
2. Select the desired audiobook from the list.

CHECK AND MANAGE YOUR CALENDAR ON APPLE WATCH
VIEW CALENDAR EVENTS
1. Open the Calendar app on your Apple Watch.
2. Turn the Digital Crown to scroll through upcoming events.
3. Tap an event to view its details, including the date, time, location, guest status, and notes.
4. To return to the previous screen or the next event, tap the "Back" button in the upper left corner.

CHANGE EVENT VIEW
1. Open the Calendar app on your Apple Watch.
2. Tap the "More Options" button.
3. Select your preferred view option, such as "Coming Soon," "List," "Day," "Week," or "Month."

VIEW WEEKS AND MONTHS FROM DAY OR LIST VIEW
1. When viewing events in Day or List view, you can switch to Week or Month view.
2. Open the Calendar app on your Apple Watch.
3. To show the current week, tap the "Back" button in the top left corner.
4. To see a different week, swipe left or right.
5. To view events for a specific week, tap a day in the weekly calendar.
6. To view the current month in the weekly view, tap the "Back" button.
7. To view a different month, turn the Digital Crown.
8. To select a specific week in your monthly calendar, tap that week.

ADD AN EVENT
1. To add an event, you can use Siri by saying, "Create a Calendar event called 'FaceTime with Mom' for May 20 at 4:00 p.m."
2. Or open the Calendar app on your Apple Watch.
3. While viewing events in Upcoming Events, Day, or List views, tap the More Options button, then tap Add.
4. Add event details such as name, location, date, and time, choose the calendar you want to add the event to, then tap the checkbox to confirm.

DELETE OR MODIFY AN EVENT
1. To delete an event you've created, tap the event, then tap "Delete" and confirm.
2. If it's a repeating event, you can choose to delete only the selected event or all future events.
3. To edit an event, tap the event, tap Edit, make your changes, then tap the checkbox to confirm.

RESPOND TO A CALENDAR INVITATION
- You can respond to calendar invitations when you receive them or later.

- If you see the invitation when you receive it, scroll to the bottom of the notification and tap "Accept," "Decline," or "Maybe."
- If you notice the notification later, tap it in the notification list, then swipe and reply.
- If you're already in the Calendar app, tap the event to reply.

For more specific actions or to contact an event organizer, see the relevant options in the Calendar app on Apple Watch.

USE THE COMPASS ON YOUR APPLE WATCH

Determine the direction, location, and altitude, depending on the model. Here's how to navigate through the various views and features:

Note: If you remove the Compass app from your iPhone, it will also be removed from your Apple Watch.

SELECT A VIEW

The Compass app on Apple Watch SE, Series 6, and later offers four different views. When you open the app for the first time, you'll see a compass indication with waypoints. You can rotate the Digital Crown down to see a large downward arrow, rotate it up twice to view the tilt, altitude, and coordinates, and keep rotating it to see waypoints such as parking location, last cellular connection point, and emergency SOS availability. In addition, all compass screens have an Altitude button for a 3D view of elevation changes for waypoints.

VIEW COMPASS DETAILS

In the Compass app, tap the Info button in the top left to check bearing, tilt, altitude, and coordinates, including latitude and longitude. In addition, you can view waypoints, add a bearing, and set an altitude change alert.

CHECK OUT I WAYPOINT

In watchOS 10, you can access waypoints created in the Compass app and guides in the Maps app. To do this, open the Compass app on your Apple Watch, tap the Compass icon, and then tap the Info button in the top left. From there, you can access and view the "Compass Waypoints," which include waypoints you've created and auto-generated waypoints, such as parking location and the last known cell phone and emergency SOS locations.

Please note that some features such as emergency call coordinates and waypoints may not be available in all areas.

VIEW AND ADD WAYPOINTS ON APPLE WATCH

You can add and view compass waypoints on your Apple Watch, which allows you to track the distance, directions, and relative altitude for each waypoint. Here's how to create and interact with compass waypoints.

CREATE COMPASS WAYPOINTS

Create a waypoint in the Compass app by opening it, tapping Waypoints, adding details, and confirming. To view waypoints, tap or select one on the Compass screens to get information about distance, orientation, and altitude.

CREATE DESTINATION WAYPOINTS

1. You can convert a waypoint to a destination to check its distance, direction, and relative elevation gain.
2. Open the Compass app on your Apple Watch.
3. Tap the Info button, tap the waypoints, and choose a waypoint or compass waypoints.
4. Scroll down and select "Create Destination Waypoints."
5. The screen shows the distance, direction, and relative elevation gain for that waypoint.

USE THE ALTITUDE DIAL

1. On Apple Watch SE, Apple Watch Series 6, and later with watchOS 10, you can view waypoint elevation changes relative to your altitude.
2. Open the Compass app on your Apple Watch.
3. From the Compass screen, tap the Altitude button at the bottom.
4. Waypoints are displayed on a watch face with icons indicating their altitude relative to your location. Smaller icons represent lower odds, while larger icons indicate higher odds.

CELLULAR NETWORK AND WAYPOINTS FOR EMERGENCY CALLS

- Cellular waypoints show the approximate most recent or closest location where your Apple Watch or iPhone connected to your carrier's cellular network.
- Emergency call waypoints indicate the approximate most recent or closest location where the device has detected the possible availability of service by an operator to make an emergency call.
- Note that the availability of waypoints can be affected by various factors, and reconnection may not always be possible near these waypoints.
- Cellular waypoints require iPhone with iOS 17, Apple Watch SE, or Apple Watch Series 6 and later with a cellular plan and watchOS 10.
- Waypoints for emergency calls are only available in the United States, Canada, and Australia.

Please note that waypoint availability may vary depending on location and circumstances.

USING RETRACE YOUR PASSES ON APPLE WATCH

You can use the Retrace Your Steps feature on Apple Watch SE, Apple Watch Series 6, and later to plot your route in reverse and find your way back if you get lost. Here's how to use this feature:

Retrace your steps:

1. Note that "Backtrack" is intended for use in remote environments, away from familiar locations such as your home or workplace, and where Wi-Fi connectivity may not be available.
2. Open the Compass app on your Apple Watch by tapping the Compass icon.
3. Tap the "Retrace Your Steps" button to start the route tracking process, then tap "Start" to start recording your route.
4. To retrace your steps, tap the Pause button, then select Retrace Steps.
5. The compass will display the location where the "Retrace Your Steps" button was initially pressed.

6. Follow the reverse path on the compass to return to the starting point where you turned on Retrace Your Steps.
7. When you have successfully retraced your route and no longer need it, tap the "Retrace Your Steps" button, then select "Delete Steps" to clear the recorded data.

USING APPLE WATCH TO FIND DEVICES

The Find Devices app on your Apple Watch is a useful tool for locating lost Apple devices.

TURN ON FIND MY NETWORK ON APPLE WATCH

If you paired your Apple Watch with your iPhone, Find My iPhone is set up automatically. To make sure you can locate your Apple Watch even when it's turned off or disconnected, make sure the Find My network is enabled.
1. Go to the Settings app on your Apple Watch.
2. Tap your name, then scroll down until you locate "Apple Watch."
3. Select the name of your Apple Watch and choose Find My Apple Watch.
4. If you haven't enabled it yet, turn on the Find My network.

For more details about setting up Find My on other Apple devices, see the Apple Support article titled "Set up Find My on your iPhone, iPad, iPod touch, or Mac."

VIEWING A DEVICE'S LOCATION

The Find Devices app on Apple Watch lets you see the location of your devices. Device Finder can find the location of your device, even if it's turned off or in various low-power modes.
1. Open the Find Devices app on your Apple Watch and tap the device you want.
2. If your device can be located, it will appear on the map, showing its approximate location, distance, time of last Wi-Fi or cellular connection, and battery level above the map.
3. If the device cannot be located, it will indicate "No location" under the device name. You can enable notifications so that they are notified when it is found.

For other family members' devices, scroll down and tap Show Family Devices.

RING APPLE DEVICES

You can use your Apple Watch to ring your iPhone, iPad, Mac, or another Apple Watch.
1. Launch the Find Devices app on your Apple Watch and select the device you want.
2. Tap "Play."
3. If your device is online, it will start making a sound after a short delay, gradually increasing in volume and lasting about two minutes. The device will also vibrate (if applicable) and a "Find My [device]" alert will appear on the screen.
4. A confirmation email will be sent to your Apple ID email address.

PLAYING YOUR AIRPODS OR BEATS HEADPHONES

If your AirPods or Beats are connected to your Apple Watch, you can use Find Devices to make them play a sound.

1. Open the Find Devices app on your Apple Watch and choose the device you want.
2. Tap "Play." For supported AirPods models, you can turn them off one at a time by tapping Left or Right.
3. If your device is online, it will immediately start playing a sound for two minutes.
4. A confirmation email will be sent to your Apple ID email address.

GET DIRECTIONS FOR A DEVICE

You can use the Maps app on your Apple Watch to get directions to a device's current location.
1. Open the Find Devices app on your Apple Watch and select the device you want to get directions for.
2. Tap "Directions" to open Maps.
3. Follow the provided route to get directions from your current location to your device's location.

RECEIVE NOTIFICATIONS WHEN YOU LEAVE A DEVICE

To avoid losing your device, you can set notifications to alert you when you move away from it. You can also establish safe places where you won't receive notifications.
1. Open the Find Devices app on your Apple Watch.
2. Choose the device you want to set notifications for.
3. Under Notifications, tap Notify Me When I Walk Away, then enable the notification.

You can also use the Find My app on your iPhone for these features.

LOCATE AN AIRTAG OR OTHER OBJECT WITH OBJECT FINDER

You can use the Find Items app on your Apple Watch to track a lost AirTag or other third-party item associated with your Apple ID.

Refer to the iPhone User Guide to learn how to set up an AirTag on your iPhone and how to add or update a third-party item in the Find My app on your iPhone.

DISPLAYING THE POSITION OF AN OBJECT

1. Open the Find Items app on your Apple Watch, then tap the item you want to locate.
2. If the object is locatable, its location will be displayed on the map, indicating where it is. Above the map, you'll see the approximate distance to your device, the last time it connected to a Wi-Fi or cellular network, and the battery charge level. An approximate location is displayed below the map.
3. If the object cannot be located, you will be shown its last known location and the time it was last detected. Under Notifications, tap "Notify When Found" and enable this feature. You will be notified when it is detected again.

MAKE THE OBJECT MAKE A SOUND

If the object is nearby, you can turn on a sound to help you locate it.
1. Open the Find Items app on your Apple Watch, then tap the object you want to play.
2. Tap "Play."
3. If you want to stop the audio before it stops automatically, tap "Stop."

GET DIRECTIONS TO AN OBJECT
You can get directions to your current location or an item's last known location in the Maps app on your Apple Watch.
1. Open the Find Items app on your Apple Watch, then tap the object you want to get directions for.
2. Tap "Directions" to launch Maps.
3. Follow the provided route to get directions from your current location to the item's current location.

RECEIVING NOTIFICATIONS WHEN YOU MOVE AWAY FROM AN OBJECT
To avoid losing an item, you can set up notifications that alert you when you move away from it. You can also establish safe locations where notifications won't be triggered.
1. Open the Find Items app on your Apple Watch.
2. Tap the item for which you want to set up a notification.
3. Tap Notify Me When I Walk Away, then enable Notify Me When I Walk Away.

Alternatively, you can open the Find My app on your iPhone, select "Items," choose the item you want to set a notification for, tap "Notify Me When I Walk Away," and turn on "Notify Me When I Walk Away." You can also add a safe location by selecting it from the suggested locations or creating a new one on the map.

Mark an AirTag or other item as lost with Find Items on Apple Watch

ENABLING LOST MODE
1. Open the Find Items app on your Apple Watch and tap the item you want to mark as lost.
2. Select "Lost Mode" and then turn on Lost Mode.

By enabling Lost Mode, you allow anyone who comes across your item to access relevant information by connecting to it. For details, see "View details of an unknown object in Find My on iPhone" in the iPhone User Guide.

DISABLING LOST MODE FOR AN ITEM
Once you've located the item, you can turn off Lost Mode:
1. Open the Find Items app on your Apple Watch and tap the item in question.
2. Go to Lost Mode and turn it off.

This will disable lost mode for the item.

MANAGE YOUR HOME WITH APPLE WATCH

MONITOR THE STATUS OF YOUR HOME
1. Launch the Home app.
2. Scroll through the available options:
    *   **Cameras:** View video feeds from up to four cameras at the top of the screen. Tap a camera to access its live stream.

- **Categories:** Browse accessories categorized under Lights, Security, Climate, Speakers, or Water. These accessories are organized by room, and those that need attention are indicated with a numeric badge. Tap a category to check or get information about the accessories in it.
- **Relevant accessories: Quickly** access relevant scenes and accessories that align with the time of day or your specific needs.

CONTROL YOUR SMART ACCESSORIES AND SCENES:
- To control an accessory:
  - Turn it on or off: Simply tap the accessory (for example, a light) or, if you have a compatible lock, tap a house key icon.
  - Adjust settings: Tap the More options button for an accessory, and if necessary, tap Done to return to the list of accessories. The available controls depend on the type of accessory.
- Control your favorite accessories, scenes, or devices in a room by going to the Favorites, Scenes, or Rooms section and selecting the desired scene or accessory. Use the More Options button to fine-tune your settings.

View video streams: To view a camera's video stream, tap the camera on the home screen. If you have more than four cameras, tap the "+" button to see all the cameras and select the one you want. Alternatively, select a room with a camera and tap the device.

Play a scene: In the Home app on your Apple Watch, tap the scene you want to activate.

Manage multiple homes: If you've set up multiple homes, you can choose which one to display on your Apple Watch by double-tapping the back button in the Home app on your watch and selecting the home you want.

SEND AND RECEIVE MESSAGES WITH THE INTERCOM FEATURE ON APPLE WATCH
With the Home app on your Apple Watch, you can use the Intercom feature to send messages to everyone in your family group. In addition, you have the flexibility to send intercom messages to rooms or specific areas of your residence.

HERE'S HOW TO GET STARTED:

1. Launch the Home app on your Apple Watch.
2. Swipe up and locate the Intercom icon.
3. To start a message, you can say something like, "Who completed the pizza?"
4. Finish by tapping "Done."

Intercom allows you to send voice messages to HomePods and devices in your family. Use your Apple Watch to specify a HomePod or location such as "notify studio" or "alert upstairs." It simplifies communication in the home, allowing you to reach family members in different locations.

CONTROL SMART HOME ACCESSORIES REMOTELY WITH APPLE WATCH
If you have an Apple TV (3rd generation or newer) or HomePod in your home, you can conveniently access your HomeKit-enabled smart accessories even when you're on the go. These Apple TV and HomePod devices act as home hubs, allowing you to interact with your accessories remotely using your paired Apple Watch and iPhone.

HERE'S HOW TO ENABLE REMOTE ACCESS:

1. On your iPhone, go to Settings.
2. Scroll down and tap your name.
3. Select iCloud and tap Show All.
4. Turn on the home option.

It's important to make sure that you're signed in with the same Apple ID on all your devices for it to work perfectly.

If you own an Apple TV and are signed in with the same Apple ID as your iPhone, the pairing process will happen automatically, allowing you to conveniently control your HomeKit-enabled accessories remotely with the assistance of your Apple Watch and iPhone.

DISCOVER AND NAVIGATE PLACES WITH APPLE WATCH

With the Maps app on your Apple Watch, you can explore your surroundings and access directions with ease. Here's how to use this feature effectively:

USING SIRI FOR QUICK ASSISTANCE

Siri can quickly assist you with map-related tasks. Say something like:
- "Where am I?"
- "Find a bar near me."

EXPLORE YOUR SURROUNDINGS WITH "WALKING DISTANCE"

1. Open the Maps app on your Apple Watch.
2. The map shows a circular area that represents a walking distance in a few minutes.
3. Rotate the Digital Crown to adjust the radius, extending it for up to 60 minutes of walking.
4. To change the unit of measurement, touch and hold the map, scroll down, and select "Distance" under "Radius Units."

SEARCH ON THE MAP:

1. Open the Maps app on your Apple Watch.
2. Tap the Search button, then select "Search."
3. You can use the Dictation button to speak your search query, or you can use the Handwrite button for handwriting input. Some Apple Watch models support QWERTY and QuickPath keyboards for text input (availability varies by language).
4. For models that support handwriting and keyboards, swipe up from the bottom of the screen to choose the Handwriting option.

Note: Handwriting input may not be available in all languages.

FIND AMENITIES NEAR YOU

1. Open the Maps app on your Apple Watch.

2. Tap the Search button, followed by the place search button (an icon that looks like a pin).
3. Select a category such as "Restaurants" or "Parking."
4. Turn the Digital Crown to browse the results and see their location on the map.
5. Tap a result to see more information.
6. To return to the list of results, tap the back button in the top left corner.

Note: Suggestions for nearby places may not be available in all areas.

LOCATION OF HIKING TRAILS

1. You can use the Maps app to discover hiking trails in the United States, complete with information such as trail name, length, elevation, and proximity to your current location.
2. Open the Maps app on your Apple Watch.
3. To find nearby trails:
   - Tap the Search button and type "trails".
4. To explore the trails in other locations:
   - Look for a different area on the map, tap the Search button, and search for "Trails." The map will show nearby hiking trails.
   - Or use Siri and ask, "Find trails in Yosemite."
5. Nearby trails are marked as green dots on the map, with trail names at the bottom of the screen.
6. Turn the Digital Crown to browse the available routes and tap a result for more details.
7. You can also tap on the map, zoom in, and select a green dot to learn more about a specific trail.

ACCESS TO GUIDES

1. On your iPhone, open the Maps app, tap the search field, swipe up, and do any of the following:
   - Tap an option under "City Guides" or "Favorite Guides."
   - Explore guides and tap a cover under Explore Guides.
   - Select an entry in Browse by Publisher and tap a cover.
   - Swipe up and tap the "Add" button next to a place name to choose a guide or create a new one.
2. Open the Maps app on your Apple Watch, tap the Search button, scroll down, and select the guide with the location you added.
   - Note: Guide availability may vary by location. Refer to your iPhone User Guide to set up and save guides in Maps.

VIEWING RECENT PLACES

1. Open the Maps app on your Apple Watch.
2. Tap the Search button, scroll down, and select a location listed under "Recents."
3. Recent entries can also include guides that you've recently viewed on your iPhone.

NAVIGATE MAPS ON APPLE WATCH

Learn how to efficiently use the Maps app on your Apple Watch to explore places, access details about different places, and work with map pins.

EXPLORING AND MANIPULATING THE MAP

- Move around the map: just drag with one finger.
- Zoom in or out of the map: Rotate the Digital Crown.
- Zoom in on a specific point: Double tap the map you want to focus on.
- Return to your current location: Tap the Location button at the bottom left of the screen.

ADDING, REPOSITIONING, AND REMOVING PINS ON THE MAP

- To insert a pin: Touch and hold the map at the location you want. When the Maps settings screen appears, scroll down and select "Insert a pin." Alternatively, you can insert a pin in your current location by tapping the blue dot and choosing "Insert Placemark."
- Replacing a placeholder: If necessary, you can insert a new placemark in a different location.

- Remove a pin: Tap to display the inserted placemark screen, then select the Trash button.

GET DIRECTIONS WITH APPLE WATCH

Learn how to get directions on your Apple Watch, whether you're driving, biking, walking, or using public transit. Siri can also help you find your way with voice commands.

SELECTION OF PREFERRED MEANS OF TRANSPORT
- Open the Maps app on your Apple Watch.
- Tap the Search button.
- Swipe through Favorites, Recents, Find Nearby, or Guides.
- Tap an entry, select a destination, then choose the corresponding option for driving, walking, biking, or transiting directions.

FOR DIRECTIONS
- Tap the directions button.
- Turn the Digital Crown to explore suggested routes.
- Select one for turn-by-turn directions.

FOR CYCLING DIRECTIONS
- Tap the bike directions button.
- Turn the Digital Crown to browse suggested routes.
- Select one for turn-by-turn directions.

FOR WALKING DIRECTIONS
- Tap the walking directions button.
- Turn the Digital Crown to choose from the suggested routes.
- Select one for turn-by-turn directions.

FOR PUBLIC TRANSPORT DIRECTIONS
- Tap the directions button.
- Turn the Digital Crown to browse suggested routes.
- Select one for step-by-step directions.

DURING THE TRIP
- Scroll down and up to see directions for different segments of the route.
- Swipe up to see an estimate of how long your route will take.

LISTENING TO THE DIRECTIONS
- When you follow directions in the car, bike, or on foot, Apple Watch provides audible and haptic feedback to let you know when to turn. A low-to-high sound pattern (tock tick, tock tick) indicates a right turn, while a high-low pattern (tick toc, tick toc) indicates a left turn.

- You will also receive vibrations as you approach and reach your destination.

Note: Location tracking must be enabled to use turn-by-turn directions. To enable or disable location tracking on your Apple Watch, go to Settings > Privacy & Security > Location Services.

USING THE MEMOJI APP ON APPLE WATCH

With the Memoji app, you can create your own custom alter ego on your Apple Watch. You have the freedom to select your skin tone, add details such as freckles, hairstyles, facial features, or accessories such as hats and glasses. Plus, you can create multiple Memojis to match your various moods.

CREATING A MEMOJI

1. Launch the Memoji app on your Apple Watch.
2. If this is your first time using the Memoji app, choose "Get Started."
3. If you've already created a Memoji, swipe up, then tap the Add Memoji button to create a new one.
4. Explore the different features and use the Digital Crown to make selections for your Memoji. Whether it's a unique haircut or trendy accessories, you can bring your alter ego to life.
5. Tap "Add" to embed the Memoji in your collection.

These Memoji you create can be used as Memoji stickers in your messages.

To create a new Memoji, tap Add Memoji, then customize it with your favorite features.

EDITING MEMOJI AND MORE

1. Open the Memoji app on your Apple Watch, select a Memoji, and choose an option:
   - To edit a Memoji: Choose facial features such as eyes or headgear, and use the Digital Crown to make selections from various choices.
   - To create a Memoji face: Scroll down and choose Create Face.
   - Go back to the watch face and swipe left to view it. This watch face will also be added to your collection within the iPhone Watch app.
   - To duplicate a Memoji: Scroll down and tap Duplicate.
   - To delete a Memoji: Scroll down and select "Delete."

MANAGE MESSAGES ON APPLE WATCH

In the Messages app on your Apple Watch, you can conveniently review incoming text messages, and you have several options for replying: dictate or handwrite a reply, send an emoji or quick reply, type a reply on a QWERTY or QuickPath keyboard (available on supported models and languages), or switch to your iPhone for a more detailed reply.

READ A MESSAGE ON APPLE WATCH

1. When you hear haptic feedback or an alert sound indicating a new message, simply pick up your Apple Watch to read it.
2. To navigate through the message, turn the Digital Crown. If you want to skip to the beginning of the message, tap the top of the screen.
   - Tip: For web links within a message, tap to see web-formatterouted content optimized for your Apple Watch. Double-tap to zoom in.
3. In case you received the message a while ago, tap and hold the top of the screen, then swipe down to access the notification. You can mark the message as read by scrolling down and tapping "Close." To dismiss the notification without marking it as read, press the Digital Crown.

ACCESSING MEDIA FILES IN A MESSAGE

Messages can include various types of media, such as photos, audio, music, and videos. Here's how to access it on your Apple Watch:
- Photos: Tap the photo to view it. Double-tap to enter full-screen mode and drag it to reposition it. To share the photo, tap it, tap "Share" and choose a sharing option or tap "Save Image" to store it in the iPhone Photos app.
- Audio clip: Tap the audio clip to play it. You can keep it by tapping "Keep" below the clip; otherwise, it will be deleted after two minutes.

- Music: If someone shares music from Apple Music through Messages, tap the song, album, or playlist to open and play it in the Music app on Apple Watch (requires an Apple Music subscription).
- Video: Tap a video to start it in full screen. Tap once to bring up the playback controls, double tap to resize, and use the crown to adjust the volume. You can return to the conversation by swiping or tapping the "Back" button. To save the video, open the message in the Messages app on your iPhone.

SENSITIVE CONTENT DETECTION
You can choose to detect and obscure sensitive content in your photos and videos before you view them on your Apple Watch. Here's how:
1. On your iPhone, go to Settings > Privacy & Security.
2. Select "Sensitive Content Warning."
3. Turn on the "Sensitive Content Alert" option and make sure AirDrop, Messages, and "Video Message" are enabled.
4. When you receive an alert, tap "Show," then choose "Yes" to view the content.

SEND MESSAGES FROM APPLE WATCH
In the Messages app on your Apple Watch, you can create and send messages that include various elements such as text, images, emojis, Memoji stickers, and audio clips. Additionally, you can use Apple Pay to send money and share your location within a message.

CREATE A MESSAGE ON APPLE WATCH
1. Launch the Messages app on your Apple Watch.
2. Tap the "New Message" button located at the top of the screen.
3. Select a contact by tapping "Add Contact," choosing a contact from the list of recent conversations, or using one of these options:
    - Tap the Microphone button to search for someone in your contacts or dictate a phone number.
    - Tap the "Add Contact" button to access the full list of contacts.
    - Tap the Numeric keypad button to enter a phone number.
4. Once you've made your selection, tap "Create Message."
5. If you've set up your Apple Watch for multiple languages, you can choose a language at this point.

COMPOSING A MESSAGE
You can compose a message using various methods, typically all from a single screen. Once you've created your message, tap the "Create Message" field and embed one or a combination of these options:
- QWERTY and QuickPath keyboard: Tap characters to enter them, or use the QuickPath keyboard to scroll through available letters without moving your finger. To complete a word, simply lift your finger.
- Handwriting: Use one finger to write your message. If you need to edit the message, turn the Digital Crown to place the cursor and make your changes. Note that handwriting input is available on Apple Watch models that support QWERTY and the QuickPath keyboard.
- Dictation: Tap the Dictate button, express your message verbally, and tap "Done." You can also dictate punctuation, such as "question mark."
- Emoji: Tap the Emoji button, select a frequently used emoji, or touch and hold a category at the bottom to browse available emojis. Once you've found the symbol you want, tap on it to include it in your message.
- Text entry with iPhone: If your paired iPhone is nearby, you'll see a notification when you start composing a message. You can tap this notification to use the iOS keyboard on your iPhone to type.

CANCELING A SENT MESSAGE
You have the option to undo a recently sent message within two minutes of sending it:
1. Open the Messages app on your Apple Watch.

2. Long press the message bubble and select "Undo Send".

A confirmation that you have not sent will appear in both your conversation and the recipient's conversation. However, keep in mind that the recipient may still see the original message in the conversation if they're using a device with iOS 15.7, iPadOS 15.7, macOS 12.6, watchOS 9, or earlier.

EDITING A SENT MESSAGE

You can edit a sent message up to five times within fifteen minutes of sending it:
1. Open the Messages app on your Apple Watch.
2. Choose the conversation that contains the message you want to edit.
3. Long press the message bubble and select "Edit".
4. Make the necessary changes, then tap "Done" to send the edited message. The message will be marked as "Edited" within the conversation.

On the recipient's device, the message will be updated to reflect the changes. Both you and the recipient can tap "Edited" to view previous versions of the message. Note that SMS messages cannot be edited.

MAKE AND RECEIVE FACETIME AUDIO CALLS IN MESSAGES ON APPLE WATCH

On watchOS 10, you have the option to initiate group FaceTime audio calls directly through the Messages app on your Apple Watch.

START A FACETIME GROUP AUDIO CALL FROM A MESSAGE CONVERSATION
1. Launch the Messages app on your Apple Watch.
2. Start composing a new message or open an existing conversation. Scroll down, then choose the "FaceTime Audio" option to start a call.
3. To invite others to join the call, do one of the following:
   - Tap the "More Options" button, select "Add People," and choose a contact.
   - Tap "2 people," tap the "Add" button at the bottom of the screen, then select a contact.

RECEIVING A FACETIME AUDIO CALL

When you receive a FaceTime audio call, you have several answer options:
- Answer the call: Tap the "Answer" button to accept the call.
- Reject the call: Tap the "Reject" button to reject the call.
- Reply with a message: Tap the More Options button, then select a default reply. Alternatively, tap "Customize," choose "Create Message," compose your reply, and tap "Send."
- Add another person to the call after you accept: Tap Two People, tap Add, and select a contact. You can also tap "Add People" to include someone else.
- View a recorded video message: If you can't answer the FaceTime call, the caller can leave a recorded video message, which will be sent to you. To view the message, tap the notification when it arrives or join the Messages conversation later and select the video.

ADD MUSIC TO YOUR APPLE WATCH
ADDING MUSIC USING YOUR IPHONE
1. Open the Watch app on your iPhone.
2. Tap "My Watch," then select "Music."
3. In the "Playlists & Albums" section, tap "Add Music."
4. Browse the albums and playlists you want to sync to your Apple Watch and tap the "Add" button to queue the content.
   - Music is transferred when your Apple Watch is in close proximity to your iPhone.
   - Tip: Use the Music app on your iPhone to create playlists tailored to your Apple Watch, such asweplaylists. For more details, see the Apple Support article titled "How to create a playlist in the Apple Music app."

ADDING MUSIC USING YOUR APPLE WATCH (REQUIRES APPLE MUSIC SUBSCRIPTION)
1. Open the Music app on your Apple Watch.
2. From the "Listen Now" screen, navigate to the content you want to add.
   - Alternatively, go back to the "Listen Now" screen, tap "Back," select "Search," and search for music to add.
3. Choose a playlist or album, tap the More Options button, then select Add to Library.
   - A confirmation message will appear to confirm that you want to add the content.
   - Note: You can listen to music on your Apple Watch when you're connected to the Internet. To play music without an internet connection, you need to download the songs first.
   - To download music to your Apple Watch, tap the More Options button again, then choose "Download."
   - Keep in mind that downloading music when your Apple Watch isn't connected to power will consume more battery than usual.

ADD A WORKOUT PLAYLIST TO YOUR APPLE WATCH
Open the Watch app on your iPhone.
Go to "Apple Watch" and select "Workout."
Choose a playlist for your workouts, which will be added to Apple Watch > Music.
Note: The workout playlist won't play automatically if you're listening to other music or audio.

REMOVE MUSIC FROM YOUR APPLE WATCH
To free up storage space or clean up your music library, remove songs from your Apple Watch.
Check your storage status in the Settings app on your Apple Watch or the Watch app on your iPhone.
To remove music using your iPhone:
Launch the Watch app on your iPhone.
Select "Music" and use the "Edit" option to delete the songs.
To remove music using your Apple Watch (requires Apple Music subscription):
Open the Music app on your Apple Watch.
Tap "Library", then "Downloaded" and choose "Remove" for playlists or albums.
You can "Remove Download" or "Delete Music from Your Library".

PLAYING MUSIC ON APPLE WATCH

Use the Music app to listen to music directly on your Apple Watch or control music playback on your iPhone.
You can also stream music from Apple Music with a subscription.
Control playback with buttons for play, pause, next, and previous.
Adjust the volume using the Digital Crown.
Shuffle and repeat options are available.

ENHANCE YOUR MUSIC EXPERIENCE:

Customize your music library, add songs to playlists, and explore artists and albums.
Access different music options within the Music app.
Configure your network settings for streaming music over cellular data.
Tune in to the radio on your Apple Watch:
Listen to Apple Music radio stations such as Apple Music 1, Apple Music Hits, and Apple Music Country.
Explore featured and genre-based stations curated by experts.
Access options such as viewing upcoming songs, adding music to your library, and sharing songs.
Use Siri to request specific radio stations.

VIEWING NEWS ARTICLES

You can access news articles on your Apple Watch in a variety of ways:
1. Open the News app directly on your Apple Watch.
2. Tap the News complication on a watch face to access news content.
3. View the News widget on the Siri watch face to see the latest articles.
4. Tap a notification from the News app to read a specific article.

READ AN ARTICLE:

To read a news article about Apple Watch, follow these steps:
1. Open the News app on your Apple Watch.
2. Scroll through the list of available items by turning the Digital Crown.
3. Tap the article you want to read to expand it.
4. To save the article and read it later on your iPhone, iPad, or Mac, scroll to the bottom of the article and tap the Bookmark button.
5. To access the saved article on another device, follow these steps based on your device:
    - On iPhone: Open the News app, go to the tab that shows the channels you follow, tap Saved Articles, and select the story you want to read.
    - On iPad: Open the News app, go to Saved Stories in the sidebar, and select the story you want.
    - On Mac: Open the News app, click Saved Stories in the sidebar, and choose the article you want to read.

SHARING AN ARTICLE:

You can easily share a news article with others by following these steps:
1. Open the News app on your Apple Watch.
2. Scroll to the article you want to share and select it.
3. Scroll down and tap the Share button.
4. Choose one of the available sharing options to share the article with friends, family, or on social media.

 If you prefer to read articles on a larger screen, you can easily switch to your iPhone:
1. Open the News app on your Apple Watch.
2. Turn on your iPhone and access the application switcher (swipe up from the bottom or double-press the Home button, depending on your iPhone model).
3. Look for the button at the bottom of the screen that opens the News app and tap on it to continue reading the articles on your iPhone.

With these instructions, you can make the most of the News app on your Apple Watch and stay well-informed while on the go.

CHOOSE A PHOTOALBUM FOR APPLE WATCH

With the Photos app on your Apple Watch, you can conveniently browse images from the specific iPhone albums you've selected, featured photos, and images from your memories.

Initially, when you start using your Apple Watch, the "Favorites" album (containing the photos you've marked as favorites) appears by default. However, you can easily switch to another photo collection.

Here's how:
1. Sign in to the Watch app on your iPhone: Launch the Watch app on your iPhone.
2. Go to the photo album settings: Tap My Watch, then go to Photos > Sync Albums.
3. Select your album: Choose the album you want to view on your Apple Watch from the available options.

If you want to remove a specific photo from your Apple Watch, open the Photos app on your iPhone and delete the image from the album you synced. To create a new album exclusively for Apple Watch photos, you can do so using the Photos app on your iPhone.

VIEW FEATURED PHOTOS AND MEMORIES ON APPLE WATCH

Your Apple Watch can automatically sync "Featured Photos" and "Memories" photos from your iPhone's photo library.
To enable this feature, follow these steps:
1. Access the Watch app on your iPhone: Open the Watch app on your iPhone.
2. Go to Photo Settings: Tap My Watch, then select Photos.
3. Enable photo syncing: Turn on Sync Memories and Sync Featured Photos.

<u>**DISABLING PHOTO SYNC**</u>

If you decide you no longer want your iPhone to sync "Memories," "Featured Photos," or images from your chosen albums to your Apple Watch, you can easily disable this feature:

1. Access the Watch app on your iPhone: Open the Watch app on your iPhone.
2. Go to Photo Settings: Tap My Watch, then go to Photos.
3. Turn off photo syncing: Simply turn off Photo Sync.

<u>**MANAGE PHOTO STORAGE ON APPLE WATCH**</u>

The number of photos your Apple Watch can store depends on how much free space you have. To make room for other content such as music or apps, you can limit the number of photos stored on your device.
Here's how:

1. Access the Watch app on your iPhone: Open the Watch app on your iPhone.
2. Go to Photo Storage Settings: Tap "My Watch," then go to "Photos" > "Photo Limit."
3. Check your photo count: To see how many photos are currently stored on your Apple Watch, you can go to the "Settings" app on your watch and go to "General" > "About," or open the Watch app on your iPhone, tap "My Watch," and visit "General" > "About."
4. Monitor photo storage: To monitor how much space your photos are taking up, go to the "Settings" app on your Apple Watch and go to "General" > "Storage." On your iPhone, you can find this information in the Watch app by selecting "My Watch" and navigating to "General" > "Storage."

ADD PODCASTS TO YOUR APPLE WATCH

You can add podcasts to your Apple Watch to listen to them wherever you are, whether or not your iPhone is nearby. You can add episodes through the Watch app on your iPhone or directly on your Apple Watch. When you use your iPhone, you can add episodes from podcasts and stations you follow in the Podcasts app. You can also follow or unfollow podcasts directly on your Apple Watch. Once added and downloaded, you can play podcasts on your watch, stored, or streamed if connected to your iPhone, Wi-Fi, or cellular service. Siri can help you play specific podcasts, and you can manage playback with various controls. You can also customize the podcast settings on your Apple Watch, including download preferences and playback options.

SET AND MANAGE REMINDERS ON APPLE WATCH

Apple Watch lets you create and respond to reminders efficiently. Here's how to set up, view, and manage reminders on Apple Watch:

VIEWING REMINDERS

1. Open the Reminders app on your Apple Watch.
2. Tap a list to view its contents.
3. To mark a reminder as complete, tap the Reminder Completed button on the left side of the item. Alternatively, tap the reminder itself, then tap Completed.
4. To return to the list view, tap the "Back" button located in the upper left corner.
5. To see completed reminders in a list, select the list, choose View Options, and tap Show Completed.
6. For an overview of all completed reminders, go to the "Completed" list, which organizes reminders by last 7 days, last 30 days, and month.
7. You can rearrange the order of your lists by going to the Reminders app on your iPhone, tapping "More Options," selecting "Edit Lists," and dragging the desired list to a new location.
8. You can also collaborate on shared lists with iCloud users. While you can join a shared list on your Apple Watch, you can't create a shared list directly from your watch.

CREATING A REMINDER

You can easily create reminders using Siri or manually in the Reminders app:

1. Using Siri: Simply say, "Remind me of [your reminder] at [specific time]." Siri will create the reminder for you.
2. Manual creation: To manually create a reminder in the Reminders app, scroll to the bottom of any list and tap Add Reminder.

DELETING A REMINDER

To delete a reminder, follow these steps:
1. Open the Reminders app on your Apple Watch.
2. Tap the list containing the reminder you want to delete.
3. Do one of the following:
   - Swipe the reminder to the left, then tap the Trash button.
   - Tap the reminder, scroll down, tap "Delete," and confirm the action.

EDITING A REMINDER

You can change reminders on your Apple Watch by following these steps in the Reminders app:

Open the Reminders app.

Tap the list containing the reminder you want to edit.

Select the specific reminder you want to edit.

Tap "Edit" to make various changes, such as renaming, adding notes, setting date and time, adding tags, location reminders, flagging, changing priority, or assigning to a different list.

These editing options give you the flexibility to customize your reminders as needed.

SETTING TIMERS ON APPLE WATCH

The Timer app on Apple Watch is a useful time management tool, allowing you to create and track various timers, each up to 24 hours long.

USING SIRI TO SET A TIMER:

You can quickly set a timer using Siri by saying "Set a timer for 20 minutes."

QUICK START A TIMER

1. Launch the Timer app on your Apple Watch.
2. For a quick timer setting, tap a predefined duration (e.g., 1, 3, or 5 minutes) or select a timer you've recently used from the "Recents" section.
3. If you prefer a custom timer, tap the "Add" button.
4. When a timer ends, you can tap the "Repeat Timer" button to start a timer of the same length.

PAUSE OR STOP A TIMER

While a timer is active, open the Timer app on your Apple Watch.
- Tap the "Pause" button to temporarily pause the timer.
- To resume a paused timer, tap the "Start" button.
- To stop a timer entirely, tap the "Done" button.

CREATING A CUSTOM TIMER

1. Sign into the Timer app on your Apple Watch.
2. Tap the "Add" button.
3. Select the hours, minutes, or seconds by tapping them, then use the Digital Crown to adjust the values.
4. Tap "Start" to start the custom timer.

SETTING MULTIPLE TIMERS

1. Launch the Timer app on your Apple Watch.
2. Create and start a timer as needed.

RECORD AND PLAY VOICE MEMOS ON APPLE WATCH

REGISTRATION

Open Voice Memos.
Tap "Record" to get started.
Tap "Stop Audio Recording" to finish.

REPRODUCTION

Open Voice Memos.
Select the reminder.
Tap "Play."
Use the "Go Forward" and "Go Back" buttons to navigate.
For more options, tap More Options.
Voice memos sync across all your Apple devices.

ADDITIONAL FEATURES ON APPLE WATCH

Playing music
Listening to audiobooks
Listen to podcasts.
Using Now Playing

USING THE WALKIE-TALKIE ON APPLE WATCH

Open Walkie-Talkie.
Invite friends to join.
To speak, touch and hold the Speak button.
Adjust the volume using the Digital Crown.

Enable "Tap to Talk" to speak with a tap.

Remove contacts by swiping left.

Change your availability in Control Center or app settings.

Note: Both participants must connect via Bluetooth, Wi-Fi, or cellular. Availability of Walkie-Talkie varies by region. Explore.

CHECK THE WEATHER ON APPLE WATCH

You can use the Weather app on your Apple Watch to check detailed weather conditions, forecasts, and various metrics. It includes information on temperature, precipitation, wind speed, UV index, visibility, humidity, and air quality. Siri can also provide quick weather updates.

TO CHECK THE LOCAL WEATHER

Open the Weather app on your Apple Watch.

Scroll to see upcoming 24-hour forecasts and extended 10-day forecasts.

You can view individual metrics by tapping the Weather button and selecting a metric. To scroll through the metrics, tap the screen. Weather alerts can be viewed during significant weather events with additional information available by tapping "More Information." Make sure location services are enabled for accurate data.

USING VOICEOVER ON APPLE WATCH

VoiceOver is a valuable accessibility feature of Apple Watch that provides assistance to users with visual impairments, allowing them to effectively use the device through voice guidance and intuitive gestures. Here's how to use VoiceOver on Apple Watch:

ENABLE OR DISABLE VOICEOVER
1. Open the Settings app on your Apple Watch.
2. Go to Accessibility > VoiceOver.
3. Turn the VoiceOver switch on or off to enable it. To turn off VoiceOver, double tap the VoiceOver button.

You can also turn VoiceOver on or off using Siri by saying "Turn VoiceOver on" or "Turn VoiceOver off."

You also have the option to turn on VoiceOver on your Apple Watch using your iPhone. To do this, open the Watch app on your iPhone, select "My Watch," go to "Accessibility," and tap the "VoiceOver" option. You can also use accessibility shortcuts for this purpose.

USING VOICEOVER FOR SETUP

VoiceOver can assist you with the initial setup of your Apple Watch. To activate this feature, triple-click the Digital Crown during the setup process. For step-by-step instructions on how to set up your Apple Watch using VoiceOver, see the "Set up Apple Watch with VoiceOver" guide.

VOICEOVER GESTURES

Here are the gestures you can use to navigate and interact with your Apple Watch when VoiceOver is enabled:

- **Move around the screen:** Slide your finger across the screen to hear VoiceOver read aloud the contents of each item you touch. You can tap to select an item, or swipe left/right to choose adjacent items. To explore other pages, swipe horizontally or vertically with two fingers.
- **Go back:** If you mistakenly select the wrong option, swipe the screen with two fingers and draw a "z" shape to go back.
- **Perform actions on an item:** With VoiceOver turned on, use a double tap instead of a single tap to perform actions such as opening an app, activating an option, or performing typical touch actions. To select an app icon or list item, tap it, then double tap to perform the corresponding action. For example, to turn off VoiceOver, select the VoiceOver button and double-tap anywhere on the screen.
- **Performing other operations:** Some items trigger various actions. Once you've selected an item, you'll hear "available actions." Swipe up or down to choose an action, then double tap to perform it.
- **Pause** VoiceOver: To momentarily stop reading VoiceOver, tap the screen with two fingers. Tap again with two fingers to resume.
- **Adjust VoiceOver volume:** Double-tap and hold with two fingers, then swipe up or down to adjust the volume. Alternatively, open the Watch app on your iPhone, select "My Watch," go to "Accessibility" > "VoiceOver," and adjust the slider.

USING THE VOICEOVER ROTOR

The VoiceOver rotor is a versatile tool for changing VoiceOver settings and navigating items on the screen. You can select various rotor settings such as Words, Characters, Actions, Headings, Volume, and Voice Speed. Here's how to use it:
1. With VoiceOver enabled, slide two fingers across the screen as if you were turning a knob. VoiceOver will announce the selected rotor setting.
2. Keep rotating your fingers to scroll through the available settings. Stop when you hear the option you want.

To interact with the rotor, use these gestures:
- Choosing a rotor setting: Rotate two fingers.
- Skip to the previous item or increase (depending on the rotor setting): Swipe up.
- Move to the next item or decrease (depending on rotor setting): Scroll down.

ADJUST VOICEOVER SETTINGS

You can customize VoiceOver behavior directly from your Apple Watch. To do this, open the Settings app on your Apple Watch, go to Accessibility > VoiceOver, and choose one of the following:

- Turn off VoiceOver
- Adjust the reading speed
- Set voice options: Tap Voice to configure voice, tone, and rotor settings.
- Set audio options: Tap Audio to change the volume of VoiceOver, enable or disable audio fading, or manage sounds and haptics.
- Set braille options: In the "Braille" section, customize the braille output, input, wrapping, how long alerts are displayed, and braille tables.
- Set keyboard options (for specific Apple Watch models): Pair a Bluetooth keyboard with your Apple Watch, then select Keyboards to choose feedback options, such as phonetics, typing feedback, modifier keys, keyboard interaction time, and devices.
- Turn off VoiceOver suggestions
- Navigate with the Digital Crown
- Choose to hear the name of the highlighted item when you lift your wrist
- Turn on Screen Curtain, which turns off the screen for privacy when using VoiceOver
- Read the number of seconds

USING ASSISTIVETOUCH ON APPLE WATCH

AssistiveTouch offers valuable assistance when using your Apple Watch becomes difficult due to difficulty touching the screen or pressing buttons. Leveraging the Apple Watch's built-in motion sensors, AssistiveTouch lets you answer calls, manage an on-screen cursor, and access a menu of actions with hand gestures.

Using gestures enabled by AssistiveTouch, you can perform various tasks, including, but not limited to:

- Interaction with the touchscreen
- Manipulating the Digital Crown by Presses and Rotations
- Navigating Between Screens
- Holding down the side button
- Access to Notification Center, Control Center, and App List
- Viewing apps
- Using Apple Pay
- Confirm actions by pressing the side button twice.
- Activating Siri
- Running Siri Shortcuts

TO SET UP ASSISTIVETOUCH

1. Open the Settings app on your Apple Watch.
2. Go to Accessibility > AssistiveTouch and turn on AssistiveTouch.
3. Activate gestures by tapping the corresponding switch.

For a complete guide on using gestures, you can tap "Learn More" under the Gestures option, then tap each gesture to view interactive animations that demonstrate successful execution.

Alternatively, you can set up AssistiveTouch through the Watch app on your iPhone:

1. Launch the Watch app on your iPhone.
2. Select your Apple Watch.
3. Go to Accessibility > AssistiveTouch and turn it on.

Once AssistiveTouch and Gestures are enabled, you can use the following default gestures to navigate your Apple Watch:

1. Pinch Forward: Advance Forward
2. Double Pinch Backwards: Navigate backwards
3. Tap while handing: Initiates touch actions!
4. Double press: Enter the Actions menu.

For example, if you have the Sundial face open and want to use AssistiveTouch with the Activity app:

1. Press twice to activate AssistiveTouch.
2. This will highlight the Music complication.
3. Triple-pinch to switch to the Activity complication, then pinch to select it.
4. After opening the Activity app, double press to bring up the Actions menu.
5. Perform another pinch to select the "System" action, followed by another pinch to choose the "Swipe Up" option, and conclude with a final press to confirm your selection.
6. Perform a compression to move to the next screen.
7. Pinch twice to bring up the Actions menu.
8. Perform a pinch to cycle through the actions and perform a double pinch to return.
9. Select the "Press Digital Crown" action and press to return to the watch face.

In addition, Motion Indicator lets you control your Apple Watch by tilting it up, down, left, or right. For example, to access the Stopwatch app:

1. When viewing the watch face, double press to turn on AssistiveTouch.
2. Double press once more to bring up the Actions menu.
3. This will highlight the "Digital Crown Awards" action. Press to select it, then open the home screen.
4. Press twice to enter the Actions menu again, pinch to access the "Interact" action, then press to tap it.
5. "Motion Pointer" should now be turned on. Perform a press to activate "Motion Pointer", which will display a cursor on the screen.
6. Tilt your Apple Watch to move the cursor along the bottom edge of the screen for scrolling.
7. Briefly press and hold the cursor on the Stopwatch app to open it.
8. Keep the cursor contact on the start button to select it.

TO RETURN TO THE WATCH FACE

1. Swipe twice to bring up the Actions menu.
2. Pinch to select the "Press Digital Crown" action, then pinch again to tap it.

In addition, "Quick Actions" make it easy to quickly respond to alerts on your Apple Watch. These actions include answering calls, snoozing alarms, stopping timers, starting workouts when your Apple Watch detects exercise, and taking photos in the Camera app when the viewfinder and shutter are visible. Here's how to adjust your Quick Actions settings:

1. Go to the Settings app on your Apple Watch.
2. Go to Accessibility > Quick Actions and select your preferred option.

You can configure quick actions to be always accessible, available only when AssistiveTouch is turned on, or completely disabled. You can also choose between full-look and minimal modes for displaying quick actions, with the former displaying a banner and a highlighted action button, while the latter highlights only the action button.

As you get used to quick actions, you can practice the gesture by tapping "Try."

For further customization of the AssistiveTouch experience, you can change the actions assigned to Pinch Sync, Collapse, and Gesture Pointer gestures. In addition, you can fine-tune the sensitivity settings for "Motion Pointer". To make the following changes:

1. Open the Settings app on your Apple Watch.
2. Navigate to Accessibility > AssistiveTouch.
3. Customize gestures by tapping Gestures, selecting a gesture, and choosing a Siri action or shortcut.
4. Customize Motion Pointer by tapping Motion Pointer and adjusting settings for sensitivity, trigger time, motion tolerance, and active edges.
5. Determine your preferred scanning style, choosing between automatic scanning, where actions are automatically highlighted in sequence, and manual scanning, where gestures are used to switch between actions.
6. Customize the look by enabling "High Contrast" to highlight the edge and tap "Color" to select an alternate highlight color.
7. Customize the menu by adding your favorite actions, adjusting the position and size of the Actions menu, and configuring the auto-scroll speed.
8. Enable "Confirm with AssistiveTouch" to confirm payments or other actions that require a double press of the side button.

Alternatively, you can do these customizations through the Watch app on your iPhone by tapping "My Watch," proceeding to Accessibility, > AssistiveTouch.

USE A BRAILLE DISPLAY WITH VOICEOVER ON APPLE WATCH

Apple Watch offers support for various international braille tables and displays. You have the option to connect a Bluetooth wireless braille display, which gives you access to VoiceOver output, which includes both contracted and uncontracted braille. When you edit text, the braille monitor conveniently displays the text in context, and any changes you make are seamlessly transformed from braille to printed text. You can also use a braille display with input keys to control your Apple Watch whenever VoiceOver is active.

CONNECT A BRAILLE DISPLAY

1. Activate the braille display by turning it on.
2. On your Apple Watch, go to Settings > Accessibility > VoiceOver > braille.
3. From the available options, select your preferred braille display.

For a complete list of braille displays supported by Apple Watch, you can refer to the Apple Support article titled "Braille displays supported by Apple Watch."

To adjust the braille display settings, follow these steps:

1. On your Apple Watch, go to Settings > Accessibility > VoiceOver > braille.
2. Choose one of the following parameters:
   - Outputs: This setting allows you to designate how the braille monitor is output, giving you options such as six dots uncontracted, eight dots not contracted, or braille contracted.
   - Input: Here you can specify the input method for entering braille on the monitor. Options include non-contracted six-dot, non-contracted eight-dot braille, or contracted braille. You also have the option to turn on "Machine Translation".
   - Wrap: This setting determines whether braille text wraps automatically.
   - Alert Display Duration: Adjusts how long alerts appear on the braille screen.
   - Braille Tables: Add braille tables to the Braille Tables rotor for quick access.

For more guidance and a list of common braille commands to use with VoiceOver on Apple Watch, you can refer to the Apple Support article titled "Common braille commands for VoiceOver on Apple Watch."

4- HEALTH FEATURES FOR APPLE WATCH ULTRA

View health information on the lock screen: You can set up your Apple Watch Ultra to display vital health information on the lock screen. This information, such as age, blood type, medical conditions, and allergies, can be invaluable in an emergency. For details, see "Set up and view health data on Apple Watch Ultra."

Contact emergency services: In an emergency, you can quickly contact emergency services by pressing and holding the side button on Apple Watch Ultra. Siri and Messages can also be used to get in touch with them. You can further enhance your safety by adding emergency contacts to alert friends and family. Find out more in the "Contact Emergency Services" section.

Turn on fall detection: Apple Watch Ultra offers fall detection functionality, which can automatically alert emergency services if a serious fall is detected. Learn how to manage fall detection in the "Manage fall detection on Apple Watch Ultra" section.

Use crash detection: In the event of a serious car accident, Apple Watch Ultra can automatically alert emergency services. To learn how to manage incident detection, see "Manage incident detection on Apple Watch Ultra."

Turn on the siren: Apple Watch Ultra comes with a built-in siren that can emit high-intensity sounds on various frequencies, making it an effective tool for signaling distress. To enable the siren, follow the instructions in the "Activate the siren" section.

SET UP AND ACCESS YOUR MEDICAL ID ON APPLE WATCH ULTRA

Your medical record is a repository of critical information about your health, including details about allergies and medical conditions you may have. In the event of an emergency, having access to this information can be critical. When you set up your Medical ID within the Health app on your iPhone, this vital data also becomes accessible on your Apple Watch Ultra. This is especially useful if you choose to share your medical records, as it allows your Apple Watch Ultra to transmit essential health information to emergency services when you initiate a 911 call or text or use the Emergency SOS feature (available in the US and Canada only).

In emergency situations, Apple Watch Ultra becomes a valuable tool, displaying your medical records for use by first responders who come to your aid.

To set up medical records on your iPhone, you can refer to the step-by-step instructions in the iPhone User Guide under "Set up and view medical records."

To access your Medical Records on Apple Watch Ultra, follow these simple steps:

1. Press and hold the side button on your Apple Watch Ultra until you see the sliders.
2. Slide the slider for medical records to the right.
3. Once you have accessed the necessary information, tap "Done" to exit.

Alternatively, you can also access your medical records on your Apple Watch Ultra through the Settings app by going to "SOS" and selecting "Medical Records."

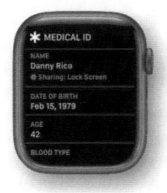

INITIATE COMMUNICATION WITH EMERGENCY SERVICES USING APPLE WATCH ULTRA.

In a critical situation, quickly call for service with your Apple Watch Ultra.

CONTACT EMERGENCY SERVICES

You can perform any of the following actions:
1. Long press the side button, then slide the Emergency Call slider to the right when the slider appears.

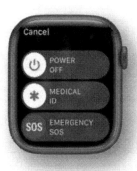

Apple Watch Ultra can contact emergency services in your area, such as 911. Please note that in some areas you may need to press and hold a number on your phone's keypad to complete the call.

Here are several ways to contact emergency services with Apple Watch Ultra:
1. Side Button Press:
    *   Press and hold the side button until your Apple Watch Ultra beeps and a countdown begins.
    *   When the countdown ends, Apple Watch Ultra will automatically call emergency services.
    *   Even if your Apple Watch Ultra is in silent mode, it will play an alert sound when the call starts.
    *   If you want to call emergency services without the countdown, use the "Emergency Call" slider.

To turn off the automatic emergency countdown:
    *   Open the Settings app on your Apple Watch Ultra.
    *   Select "SOS," then tap "Press and hold the side button."
    *   Turn off "Press and hold the side button to dial the number." You can still use the "Emergency Call" slider.
2. Voice command:
    *   You can say "Hey Siri, call 911" to initiate an emergency call.
3. Messages app:
    *   Open the Messages app on your Apple Watch Ultra.
    *   Tap New Message, then tap Add Contact.
    *   Tap the numeric keypad key and type 112.
    *   Tap "Create Message," enter your message, and tap "Send."
4. Fall Detection (if enabled):
    *   If fall detection is enabled and Apple Watch Ultra detects a serious fall, it will attempt an automated 911 call.
5. Incident detection (if supported):
    *   Apple Watch Ultra can detect serious traffic accidents and can initiate an emergency call after 20 seconds.
6. Location & Cellular Connectivity:
    *   You can make emergency calls on Apple Watch Ultra in various locations, as long as a cellular network is available.
    *   Some cellular networks might not accept emergency calls if your Apple Watch Ultra isn't turned on, isn't compatible, isn't set up for a specific network, or isn't set up for cellular service.
7. Emergency Contacts:

- You can also set up emergency contacts. After an emergency call, Apple Watch Ultra will notify your emergency contacts and send your location.
- To add emergency contacts, refer to the "Set up and view your Medical ID" section in the iPhone User Guide.

Keep in mind that when you make an "Emergency SOS" call while abroad, the watch will connect to local emergency services, but it may not send your location or text messages to your emergency contacts. Behavior may vary by country and region.

TO END AN EMERGENCY CALL

If you accidentally make an emergency call, you can cancel it by tapping the "End Call" button and then selecting the "End Call" option.

CHANGE OR UPDATE THE EMERGENCY ADDRESS

If emergency services are unable to locate you, they will use the designated emergency address.
To update this address:
1. Open the Settings app on your iPhone.
2. Go to Phone > Wi-Fi Calling.
3. Tap "Update Emergency Address" and enter your new emergency address.

TURN ON THE SIREN

Turn on the built-in siren on Apple Watch Ultra to emit high-intensity sound sequences, accompanied by wrist vibrations, to attract attention during emergencies. Here's how to activate the siren:
1. Press and hold the Actions button and wait for the countdown to end. You can tap Cancel if you change your mind and don't want the siren to go off.

Note: To prevent the siren from triggering when you press and hold the Action button, go to the Settings app on your Apple Watch Ultra, tap Action Button, and turn off "Press and Hold to Wake" in the Siren section.
2. Press and hold the side button, then swipe right on the siren slider.
3. Open the Siren app on your Apple Watch Ultra, then tap the button to turn it on.
4. You can also use voice commands by saying "Turn on the siren" and then tapping the Play button to activate it.

The siren on Apple Watch Ultra will continue to beep and vibrate on your wrist until you turn it off or the battery runs out.
WARNING: Whenever possible, avoid activating the siren near your ears or inside enclosed spaces.

MANAGE FALL DETECTION SETTINGS ON APPLE WATCH ULTRA

When fall detection is turned on, if Apple Watch Ultra detects a sudden fall, it can initiate contact with emergency services and send a message to your emergency contacts. In the event of a hard fall where you remain motionless for about a minute, Apple Watch Ultra provides haptic feedback, beeps, and attempts to contact emergency services.

To make an emergency call, a nearby Apple Watch Ultra or iPhone must have a cellular connection, or Wi-Fi must be enabled with accessible cellular coverage.

In cases where both cellular and Wi-Fi connections aren't available and an iPhone 14 or iPhone 14 Pro (or later) is in close proximity to Apple Watch Ultra, fall detection may use the iPhone to transmit the Emergency SOS notification via satellite, provided service is available. For more details, see the Apple Support article on using Emergency SOS via satellite on iPhone 14.

If the date of birth you provide when you set up your Apple Watch Ultra or enter your age in the Health app on your iPhone indicates that you're over 55, fall detection will be turned on automatically. However, if you're in the 18-55 age group, you can manually turn on fall detection by following one of the steps below:

1. Go to the Settings app on your Apple Watch Ultra.
    • Go to Emergency SOS > Fall Detection and turn on the feature.
2. Alternatively, use the Watch app on your iPhone.
    • Tap My Watch, then select Emergency SOS and enable fall detection.

It's important to note that disabling wrist tracking means that your Apple Watch Ultra won't automatically initiate emergency calls even after detecting a significant drop.

You have the option to keep "Always On" fall detection, making sure it's continuously on, or set it to "On only during workouts", which limits its activation to when you're engaged in a training session.

For people between the ages of 18 and 55 who set up a new Apple Watch with watchOS 8.1 or later, fall detection is automatically turned on only during workouts. If you're updating your Apple Watch from an earlier version of watchOS, you'll need to manually enable the "During Workouts Only" option.

Keep in mind that while fall detection is a valuable feature, it may not detect all types of falls. Increased physical activity can potentially trigger the feature, especially during high-impact workouts, as they can be interpreted as falls. For more information, see the Apple Support article Use fall detection with your Apple Watch.

CHECK INCIDENT DETECTION ON APPLE WATCH ULTRA

Use crash detection on Apple Watch Ultra for serious car accidents. If a significant car crash is detected, Apple Watch Ultra will promptly display an alert and can automatically start an emergency call after a 20-second countdown, unless you choose to cancel it. If there is no response from the user, Apple Watch will play an audio message for emergency services, relaying details about the serious traffic accident, including approximate latitude and longitude coordinates within a given search radius.

To make the emergency call, you must have a nearby Apple Watch Ultra or iPhone with an active cellular connection or a Wi-Fi enabled network with accessible cellular coverage. In situations where both cellular and Wi-Fi coverage are not available and you have an iPhone 14, iPhone 14 Pro, or later model nearby, incident detection notifications may be transmitted to emergency services using the "Emergency SOS" system via satellite, if this service is supported. For more information, see the Apple Support article on using Emergency SOS via satellite with iPhone 14.

Please note that when "Incident Detection" identifies a serious traffic accident, it will not cancel ongoing emergency calls initiated by other means.

START YOUR JOURNEY WITH APPLEFITNESS+

By subscribing to Apple Fitness+, you'll have access to a diverse library with a wide range of workouts, including HIIT, core training, muscle strengthening, yoga, cycling, and more. In addition, you can participate in guided meditations aimed at improving your overall well-being.

While you're wearing your Apple Watch during a workout, your performance metrics, such as heart rate and calorie expenditure, are seamlessly streamed to your iPhone, iPad, or Apple TV, ensuring you stay informed of your progress. These workout metrics are also synced with your daily activity data after you complete a workout.

Note that Apple Fitness+ may not be accessible in all countries or regions.

To access Apple Fitness+ and embark on your fitness journey, you must first subscribe. Start by launching the Fitness app on your iPhone, iPad, or Apple TV. If you're using a device other than an iPhone, simply tap Fitness+. Then, choose the free trial option and proceed by following the on-screen instructions.

INSTALL THE FITNESS APP

To access Apple Fitness+, it's essential that you have the Fitness app installed on your iPhone, iPad, or Apple TV. If the Fitness app is not currently on your device, you can easily get it by downloading it from the App Store.

Note that for setting up Apple TV with Apple Fitness+, you can refer to the "Set up the Fitness app on Apple TV with Apple Watch or iPhone" section in the Apple TV User Guide.

SIGN UP FOR APPLE FITNESS+

Launch the Fitness app on your iPhone or iPad. If you're not on an iPhone, simply tap on the Fitness+ option. Then, click on the free trial button and proceed by following the on-screen instructions to sign in using your Apple ID and verify your subscription.

TO SIGN IN TO APPLE FITNESS+

Sign up for Apple Fitness+ through the Fitness app on your iPhone, iPad, or Apple TV. If you subscribe to Apple One Premier, you have the option to pair your Apple Fitness+ subscription with other Apple services. For more information, see the Apple Support article titled "Apple subscription bundles with Apple One."

Note that Apple Fitness+ and Apple One Premier may not be accessible in all countries or regions. You can refer to the Apple Support article titled "Availability of Apple Media Services" for more details on availability.

REQUIREMENTS FOR SIGNING IN TO APPLE FITNESS+

Requirements for using Apple Fitness+:

1. To use Apple Fitness+ with Apple Watch, you need an Apple Watch Series 3 or later with watchOS 7.2 or later. Make sure it's paired with an iPhone 6s or later with iOS 14.3 or later.
2. If you want to enjoy Apple Fitness+ workouts without Apple Watch, you can use an iPhone 8 or later with iOS 16.1 or later. For more details about using Apple Fitness+ on iPhone, see the "Browse workouts and meditations on Apple Fitness+ on iPhone" section of the iPhone User Guide.

Keep in mind that if you choose to exercise without your Apple Watch, some personal metrics such as heart rate and calorie data may not be available.

3. While exercising with your compatible Apple Watch and iPhone, you also have the option to use Apple Fitness+ on other supported devices, including:
   - iPad with iPadOS 14.3 or later.
   - Apple TV 4K or Apple TV HD with tvOS 14.3 or later.
4. To access the latest Apple Fitness+ features and capabilities, we recommend using an Apple Watch Series 4 or later with watchOS 10, paired with an iPhone X or later with iOS 17. You can also use an iPad with iPadOS 17 and an Apple TV 4K or HDTV with tvOS 17 for the best experience.

SELECT YOUR FAVORITE WORKOUTS AND TRAINERS

When you're ready to start your workout, simply open the Fitness app, select your desired workout type, session, and preferred trainer. To facilitate the selection process, you can watch a preview of your session and access your workout details, including the playlist, music genre, subtitle availability, and required equipment. Each Apple Fitness+ trainer has its own distinct approach, musical style, and workout routines, providing a personalized touch to each session. You can also learn more about the coaches by reading their biographies and exploring the variety of workouts they offer.

REVIEW YOUR STATS

Track your progress and monitor your heart rate and calories burned while exercising with Apple Watch. Workout stats are displayed on the screen, some even include a performance bar for comparing metrics with others. Change your workout metrics by tapping the screen during a session.

DESIGN YOUR OWN PERSONALIZED TRAINING PROGRAM

Create Your Own Fitness Plan You can create a personalized fitness regimen tailored to your fitness schedule and goals. To start your custom plan, log in to Fitness+, click Create Your Plan, then specify the days you plan to exercise, the length of each workout session, and the specific activities you prefer, such as HIIT, yoga, strength training, meditations, and more.

SHARE YOUR APPLE FITNESS+ SUBSCRIPTION USING FAMILY SHARING

When you subscribe to Apple Fitness+ or Apple One Premier, you can use Family Sharing to extend your subscription to up to five other family members. Family members will not have to take any action; Apple Fitness+ will become accessible when they first open the Fitness app after subscribing (assuming they have an Apple Watch Series 4 or later). Even if a family member has an Apple Watch but not an iPhone (because their Apple Watch was set up by another family member), they can still use Apple Fitness+ with Apple TV or iPad.

Note: To stop sharing Apple Fitness+ with a family group, you can remove a member from your Family Sharing group. For more information, see "Add or remove Family Sharing members" in the iPhone User Guide.

SEARCH FOR WORKOUTS AND MEDITATION SESSIONS IN FITNESS+

Apple Fitness+ offers a variety of ways to discover workouts, meditation sessions, and routines tailored to your preferences. You can explore individual workouts or meditation sessions, start multi-part programs, categorize and refine workouts for specific types, curate collections of your favorite activities, get personalized recommendations from fitness experts, or select a suggested workout that aligns with your goals. For example, cool-down sessions last 5 minutes, while other training categories extend up to 45 minutes. Meditation sessions come in 5, 10, or 20-minute durations, and new workouts are introduced each week to keep your options different.

REFER TO THE AVAILABLE WORKOUT AND MEDITATION OPTIONS

Explore workout and meditation options in Apple Fitness+ with the following steps:
1. Open the Fitness app on your iPhone or iPad. If you're not using an iPhone, sign in to Fitness+.
2. Choose from the following options:
    - Browse by workout type: Swipe left or right to explore the different types of activities displayed at the top of the screen.
    - Access audio workouts (iPhone only): Select "Let's Walk" or "Run" workouts for audio sessions that are compatible with Apple Watch. Add an episode to your Apple Watch by tapping the "Add" button. To listen to an additional episode, open the Workout app on your Apple Watch, go to Audio Workouts, select Library, and choose the workout you want.
    - Browse featured activities: Scroll down to find categories like "New Workouts," "New Meditations," "Beginner Workouts," "Popular," or "Quick & Easy."
    - Explore content by manager: Review the list of coaches, then swipe left or right to select a coach, view their workouts, and filter by type, duration, and playlist. Tap "Show All" to see a full list of all coaches.
    - More about what you do: Learn about workouts based on the coaches you train with frequently and the types of workouts you complete on your Apple Watch or other fitness apps that work with the Health app.
    - Try something new: Find workouts that are similar to your usual routine but with different trainers and types of exercises to diversify your training.
    - View your library: Scroll down to access your library, where you can see your saved workouts, meditations, collections, and custom plans. Use "My Library" to save your favorite workouts, create routines, or save workouts for offline use.

As you navigate, workouts you've previously completed will have a checkmark icon on their thumbnails.
Tip: An Apple Fitness+ subscription gives you access to guided meditations in the Mindfulness app on your Apple Watch.

ORGANIZE YOUR WORKOUTS AND MEDITATIONS INTO COLLECTIONS

Apple Fitness+ allows you to create collections, which are essentially playlists of workouts or meditations that play sequentially. These collections allow you to design personalized workout routines that include your favorite activities. For example, you can create a collection with intense workouts followed by a relaxing cool-down meditation.

Here's how to manage your collections in the Fitness app:

1. Open the Fitness app on your iPhone or iPad. If you're using another device, go to Fitness+.
2. Choose an activity, then tap the More options button located in the top-right corner.
3. Select "Add to Collection."
4. Alternatively, you can touch and hold an activity, then choose Add to Collection.
5. Once you've added the workouts you want to your collection, tap the Collection button. Next, do one of the following:
   - To start the collection, tap the corresponding option.
   - To add the collection to your library, tap the More Options button and select "Add to Library."
   - To remove a task from your collection, swipe left on the task and tap "Delete."
   - To reorder tasks within the collection, use the Reorder button next to a task to move it up or down.
   - To delete content in a collection, tap the More options button and select Delete Library Content.

With Apple Fitness+ collections, you can create and manage personalized workout routines based on your preferences and fitness goals.

ASK THE TEAM OF TRAINERS FOR ADVICE

Access coach tips to improve health and fitness.

By subscribing to Apple Fitness+, you'll have access to short videos that offer valuable tips to help you maintain an active and mindful lifestyle, improve your training techniques, and stay on track with your fitness goals.

Please note that these recommendations from the training team may not be accessible in all countries or regions.

Here's how to access it:

1. Open the Fitness app on your iPhone or iPad. If you're not using an iPhone, go to Fitness+.
2. Scroll down to find trainers' recommendations and select the content you want to watch.
3. You can also choose "Show All" to see the full list of suggestions.

Keep in mind that a new tip is added every week to keep you informed and motivated.

ORGANIZE AND REFINE YOUR TRAINING AND MEDITATION SELECTIONS

Customize your workout experience with sorting and filtering.

The Apple Fitness+ interface offers an intuitive way to customize your workout choices. You can easily sort and filter workouts according to your preferences. Here's how:

1. Start by launching the Fitness app on your iPhone or iPad. If you're not using an iPhone, simply tap Fitness+.
2. At the top of the screen, you'll see a list of coaches, followed by time frames displayed in the middle of the screen. Below the time frames, there is a selection of music genres.
3. Select the type of workout you're interested in, then choose one of the following options:
   - To sort tasks: Tap the "Sort" button and choose an option like Coach or Time.
   - To apply filters: Tap the "Filter" button and select the filters that best suit your preferences.

Keep in mind that if you can't select filters, it means there are no matching workouts based on your chosen criteria.

EXPLORE MULTI-PART WORKOUT AND MEDITATION PROGRAMS

Here are the detailed steps to explore workout and meditation programs on Apple Fitness+:

1. Start by opening the Fitness app on your iPhone or iPad. If you're using a device other than an iPhone, tap the Fitness+ option.
2. Depending on your preference, you can choose between Workout Programs or Meditation Programs. Just scroll down to the respective category and tap on "Show All".
3. Browse through the available programs, and when you find one you're interested in, tap on it. Each box in the program provides information about the types of workouts or meditations it includes and the number of episodes.
4. At this point, you have several options:
   - Program preview: By tapping "Watch Movie," you can watch a video that introduces the program's goals and the types of workouts or meditations it offers. For more detailed information, you can also read the schedule.
   - Add episodes to your library: If you want to save specific episodes, tap the "Add" button next to the episode you want, or use the "Add All" button at the bottom of the screen to add all episodes of the show to your library.
   - Start a program episode: To start a workout or meditation session, select an episode from the list, then tap the Start Workout button.
   - After you've completed one episode, the next one will automatically appear under "Next Workout" to help you keep up your pace. However, you can choose any episode of the program at any time.

Note that Apple Fitness+ availability may vary by country or region.

TO START A WORKOUT OR MEDITATION SESSION WITH APPLE FITNESS+

1. Open the Fitness app on your device. If you're not using an iPhone, tap the Fitness+ option.
2. At the top of the screen, select the type of activity you're interested in, such as HIIT, yoga, or strength training.
3. Choose a specific workout or meditation from the available options, or explore content in categories such as Popular or Guest Trainer Series.
4. There are several options available:
   - Add the selected activity to your library by tapping the "Add Session" button.
   - Preview the task to get an idea of what it entails by tapping "Preview."
   - Review the activity playlist. If you subscribe to Apple Music, you can listen to the associated playlist by tapping "Listen to Music."
5. To start the activity, tap the start activity button, then tap the "Play" button on your iPhone, iPad, or Apple Watch. If you're starting a treadmill workout, select "Run" or "Walk" to ensure accurate metrics, especially if you're using a treadmill.

6. If you don't wear an Apple Watch but still want to work out, you can choose to start your workout without it. Keep in mind that some metrics, such as calories burned, won't be collected in this case. Tap "Workout without Apple Watch" to proceed.
7. If you want to cast your workout to an AirPlay 2.0-compatible device, such as a TV or HomePod, tap the screen during the workout, then tap the AirPlay button and select your preferred destination.
8. Apple Fitness+ workouts also include additional trainers that show variations and provide guidance. They can help you adjust exercises to make them easier or more challenging, and they can suggest modifications, such as performing a bodyweight version of an exercise instead of using weights.

Enjoy your Apple Fitness+ workout or meditation session with access to various activities and helpful guidance from trainers.

TO PAUSE AND RESUME A WORKOUT OR MEDITATION WITH APPLE FITNESS+

Pause an activity:
1. Press the side button and the Digital Crown at the same time. Alternatively, swipe left or right on the watch face, then tap the Pause button.

Resume an activity:
1. Press the side button and the Digital Crown at the same time again, swipe right and tap "Resume," or swipe left and tap the "Start" button.

To stop and review a workout or meditation with Apple Fitness+
1. Swipe right on the watch face while exercising or meditating.
2. Tap "Done."
3. Then, tap on "End Session."

A summary of the workout will appear, and you can tap the "Done" button to return to the Workout app. This allows you to end the session and review your performance if necessary.

PRACTICE IN GROUPS WITH SHAREPLAY

You can participate in group workouts with up to 32 people using SharePlay. Start a FaceTime call on your iPhone or iPad and use the Fitness app to start a group workout. The progress is synchronized across all devices, and anyone can control it. This allows for group motivation, tracking of activity ring closures, and notifications for performance leadership during activities such as HIIT, spinning, treadmill, or rowing.

To participate in group workouts with Apple Fitness+, you'll need specific Apple devices, including iPhone, iPad, iPod touch, or Mac, with the required operating systems. Keep in mind that availability of FaceTime features and Apple services may vary by region, and Apple Watch Series 4 or later with watchOS 8.1 or later requires you to use Apple Watch during workouts. Instructions for setting up SharePlay can be found in the User Guide for your iPhone or iPad

Change the on-screen metrics to your preference during your Apple Fitness+ workout.

As you exercise, you can track your progress for each of your activity rings in real-time on your device. If you're wearing an Apple Watch, you can also track your heart rate and calories burned.

Some workouts include a performance bar, which indicates the progress of the metric compared to others who have previously completed the same workout. As you burn more calories, your position on the performance bar will improve, and this information will be saved in your workout summary along with other metrics.

You have the flexibility to customize the Apple Watch metrics that appear on your screen during your workout. Metric preferences are synced across all Apple devices linked to your Apple ID.

Note that Fitness+ subscribers who use AirPlay to mirror their workouts to compatible screens can now access personal data in real-time from their Apple Watch.

To adjust your metrics during a workout, follow these steps:
1. Tap the Metrics button.
2. Choose one of the following options:
   - Turn off all metrics: Select "Show Metrics" to disable them. Metrics will still be collected, but they won't be displayed on the screen.

- Adjust the time display: Select between "Off", "Show elapsed time" or "Show time remaining" to customize how the time is presented during the workout.
- Disable the performance bar: Turn off "Performance Bar" if you prefer not to participate in the shared performance bar feature and avoid seeing your leaderboard at the end of the workout.

ENABLE CLOSED CAPTIONING

Apple Fitness+ offers standard captions and captions for the deaf or hard of hearing for all your workouts and meditations. You can check if a workout includes subtitles and subtitles when you select it; This information is displayed along with the duration, music genre, and date added.

During a workout, tap the More Options button, then select Subtitles and choose your preferred language.

DOWNLOAD AN APPLE FITNESS+ WORKOUT OR MEDITATION TO YOUR IPHONE OR IPAD

You have the option to download workouts and meditations to your iPhone or iPad, allowing you to train offline.

Open the Fitness app. If you're not using an iPhone, tap Fitness+.

Here are the available options:

1. Download an activity to your device:
   - Tap an activity.
   - Tap the Add button to add it to your library.
   - Then, tap on the Download button.
2. View all downloaded activities:
   - Log in to your library.
   - Select the Downloaded section.

To start a downloaded activity, choose your preferred option and start your session.

To remove a downloaded activity from your device:
- Tap the downloaded activity.
- Press the More button.
- Then, select Remove Download.

Please note that the performance bar is not available during downloaded workouts.

TRACK YOUR DAILY PHYSICAL ACTIVITY WITH THE HELP OF YOUR APPLE WATCH.

You can check your progress at any time by opening the Activity app on your Apple Watch. The Activity app shows three rings that represent different aspects of your physical activity:

1. The red Motion ring reflects the active calories burned.
2. The green Exercise ring tracks your minutes of intense activity.
3. The blue "Standing" ring keeps tabs on the times you've stood up and moved for at least one minute per hour.

If you've indicated that you use a wheelchair, the "Standing" ring turns into "Active Breaks," which record the number of one-minute active breaks you take per hour.

You can navigate through your stats by turning the Digital Crown. Swipe to see your progress for each ring, distance traveled, total distance traveled, flights of stairs climbed, and your activity history.

When the rings overlap, it means you've exceeded your daily goal. To get an overview of your progress for the week, simply tap on the "Weekly Summary" button.

CHECK YOUR WEEKLY SUMMARY

To review your weekly progress, follow these steps:
1. Launch the Activity app on your Apple Watch.
2. Tap the "Weekly Summary" button.

Here you'll find a summary that provides both your daily average and your total progress for each of the rings over the course of the week.

ADJUST YOUR GOALS

If you want to change your activity goals, if they seem too easy or too challenging, you can do so with these steps:
1. Open the Activity app on your Apple Watch.
2. Tap the "Weekly Summary" button.
3. Scroll to the bottom of the screen using the Digital Crown, then choose Edit Lenses.
4. Use the Plus (+) or Minus (-) buttons to make changes to your goals, then select "Next."
5. When you're done, tap "OK."

To customize the goals for each ring, use the Digital Crown to select a specific ring, then tap Edit Goals.

Plus, every Monday, you'll receive a notification that summarizes the previous week's results and offers goal suggestions for the coming week, based on your performance.

TAKE A LOOK AT YOUR RESULTS

If you've achieved personal bests, made continuous improvements, or reached milestones with your Apple Watch, you can earn rewards. Here's how to view all your rewards:
1. Open the Activity app on your Apple Watch.
2. Tap the "Press" button.
3. Tap on any reward to get more details about it.

You can also check the rewards you've earned by opening the Fitness app on your iPhone and scrolling down to find your results at the bottom of the screen. For more information about competitions, you can refer to the "Challenging Friends" section.

TERMINATE YOUR APPLE FITNESS+ SUBSCRIPTION

Open the Fitness app on your iPhone or iPad. If you're using an iPhone, tap "Summary." Next, tap your profile picture, followed by [account name], then select Apple Fitness+.

Simply follow the on-screen instructions to change or cancel your subscription.

If you're an Apple Fitness+ subscriber through Apple One Premier and want to cancel your subscription, see the Apple Support article titled "How to cancel an Apple subscription" for help.

CHECK YOUR BLOOD OXYGEN LEVELS WITH APPLE WATCH

Use the O_2 Levels app on Apple Watch Series 6 or later to measure the percentage of oxygen your red blood cells carry from your lungs to the rest of your body. Tracking your blood oxygen levels with this app can provide insight into your overall health and well-being. It is important to note that measurements taken with the O_2 Levels app are not intended for medical purposes.

SET YOUR $_2$ LEVELS

1. Open the Settings app on your Apple Watch.
2. Tap "O_2 Levels".
3. Turn on O_2 level measurements.

MEASURING BLOOD OXYGEN LEVELS

1. Open the O_2 Levels app on your Apple Watch.
2. Place your arm on a flat surface with your wrist facing up and the Apple Watch screen visible.
3. Tap "Start" and hold your arm steady during the 15-second countdown.
4. Once the measurement is complete, view the results and tap "Done."

Note: To ensure accuracy, make sure the back of your Apple Watch is in contact with your skin. Wear your Apple Watch comfortably, not too tight or too loose, and at wrist level for accurate measurements. For more details, see the Apple Support article on using the O_2 Levels app on Apple Watch

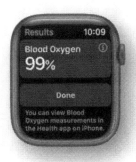

ACCESS LEVEL O_2 MEASUREMENT HISTORY

1. Open the Health app on your iPhone.
2. Select "Browse."
3. Choose "Respiratory System."
4. Tap "O_2 Levels".

CYCLE TRACKING ON APPLE WATCH

The Cycle Tracker app on Apple Watch allows you to enter and manage the details of your menstrual cycle. You can record flow information and track symptoms such as headaches and cramps. Based on the data provided, the Cycle Tracker app can alert you to the expected start of your next menstrual cycle or fertility period. In addition, you can improve your predictions using heart rate data. If you wear an Apple Watch Series 8 or Apple Watch Series 9 while you sleep, the app can also incorporate wrist temperature data to further improve cycle predictions and provide retrospective ovulation estimates. For a complete guide, see the iPhone User Guide and the Apple Support article titled "Track your period with Period Tracking."

Important note: The Health app is designed to safeguard your privacy and allow you to choose the type of data you want to share. Learn more about the privacy and data protection features of the Health app.

SETTING UP CYCLE MONITORING
1. Launch the Health app on your iPhone.
2. Tap "Browse" at the bottom right to access the Health Categories screen.
3. Select "Cycle Tracking."
4. Tap "Get Started" and follow the onscreen instructions to set up notifications and other preferences.
5. If you want to add or remove options after initially setting up cycle tracking, open the Health app on your iPhone, go to "Browse," tap "Cycle Tracking," and choose "Options" next to "Cycle Log."

ENTERING CYCLE INFORMATION
1. Open the Cycle Tracker app on your Apple Watch.
2. There are two options:
   - To record the start of your period: On the specific day of your history, tap Record. Select "Period," choose the type of flow, and tap "Done."
   - To log symptoms, spotting, or other details: On the specific day of the timeline, tap Record. Select a category, choose an option, and tap "Done."
3. The information you provide will be displayed in the menstrual cycle details on your iPhone. If you've enabled menstrual notifications and fertile window notifications in the health app on your iPhone, you'll receive alerts on your Apple Watch that alert you to upcoming periods, provide estimates of your fertile periods, and on Apple Watch Series 8 or Apple Watch Series 9, provide retrospective estimates of ovulation.

Important info: On your iPhone, you can also log specific factors in the health app that might affect your cycle, such as pregnancy, breastfeeding, and birth control use. Depending on the factors you select, menstrual cycle predictions, fertile window estimates, and, on Apple Watch Series 8 or Apple Watch Series 9, retrospective ovulation estimates may be turned off on both your iPhone and Apple Watch. For more details, see the iPhone User Guide.

GET RETROSPECTIVE OVULATION ESTIMATES (APPLE WATCH SERIES 8 AND APPLE WATCH SERIES 9 ONLY)
If you constantly wear Apple Watch Series 8 or Apple Watch Series 9 while you sleep, it can monitor changes in body temperature. This data is used to improve menstrual cycle predictions and provide retrospective ovulation estimates (please note that this feature may not be available in all regions*).

Important: It is crucial to emphasize that the "Cycle Tracker" app should not be considered a method of contraception. In addition, the data obtained from "Cycle Tracking" should not be used to diagnose any medical conditions or pathologies.

SETTING UP WRIST TEMPERATURE MONITORING
1. Set up cycle tracking and sleep.

2. To establish a baseline temperature, make sure sleep tracking is turned on and wear your Apple Watch while you sleep.
3. Pulse temperature data will be accessible after about five nights.
4. To view your wrist temperature data, go to the health app on your iPhone, go to "Browse," select "Body Measurements," and tap "Pulse Temperature."
5. Retrospective ovulation estimates should be available after two menstrual cycles during which you consistently wore your Apple Watch to bed every night.

Note: It is important to understand that body temperature fluctuates naturally and can change from one night to the next due to various factors. In addition, the temperature of your wrist can be affected by external conditions, such as the environment in which you sleep.

TO RECORD AN ECG

1. Open the Health app on your iPhone, then follow the on-screen instructions that guide you through setting up your ECG.
2. If you don't receive a setup prompt, follow these steps: Tap "Browse" in the bottom-right corner, select "Health," then tap "Electrocardiogram (ECG)."
3. Open the ECG app on your Apple Watch.
4. Rest your arm on a flat surface, such as a table or your legs.
5. With your hand on your arm that is not wearing the watch, place your finger on the Digital Crown. Wait for your Apple Watch to record the ECG. You don't need to press the Digital Crown while recording.
6. When the registration is complete, you will receive a rating. You can further document any symptoms by tapping "Add Symptoms" and selecting your symptoms. Tap "Save" to write down any symptoms, then tap "Done."
7. To view the results on your iPhone, open the health app, select "Browse" in the bottom right corner, go to "Heart," and then choose "Electrocardiogram (ECG)".

Important: To get the most accurate readings, make sure your Apple Watch is clean and dry, especially after activities such as swimming, showering, strenuous exercises that cause heavy sweating, or hand washing. It may take more than an hour for your Apple Watch to dry completely. Also, keep in mind that the ECG app is designed to operate in the temperature range of 0°C to 35°C (32ºF to 95ºF).

For more detailed information about the ECG app, see the Apple Support article titled "How to record an electrocardiogram with the ECG app on Apple Watch Series 4 or later," as well as the ECG app instruction document.

MONITOR YOUR HEART RATE WITH APPLE WATCH

Your Apple Watch provides valuable heart rate monitoring, allowing you to keep an eye on your body's performance. You can check your heart rate in various scenarios, such as during workouts, at rest, while walking, after workouts, or during breathing sessions. Here's how:

Note: Make sure both your Apple Watch and wrist are clean and dry for accurate readings. Water and sweat can affect the quality of the measurements.

CHECK YOUR HEART RATE

1. Open the Heart Rate app on your Apple Watch to instantly see your current heart rate, resting heart rate, and average walking rate.
2. Your Apple Watch continues to monitor your heart rate as long as you wear it.

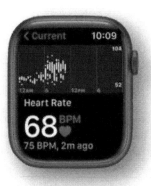

VIEW A HEART RATE GRAPH

1. Open the Heart Rate app on your Apple Watch.
2. Use the Digital Crown to navigate and select options such as "Current," "Resting Heart Rate," or "Average Walk" to review your heart rate data throughout the day.
3. For a more complete heart rate history, go to the health app on your iPhone. Go to "Browse," select "Heart," and tap an item to view data for the previous hour, day, week, month, or year.

TURN ON HEART RATE MONITORING

If you've previously disabled heart rate monitoring, you can easily turn it back on:

1. Open the Settings app on your Apple Watch.
2. Go to "Privacy & Security" > "Health."
3. Tap Heart Rate, then turn it on.
4. Alternatively, you can do this through the Watch app on your iPhone. Go to "Apple Watch" > "My Apple Watch" > "Privacy" and enable "Heart Rate Monitoring".

For more information about irregular heart rhythm notifications, see the Apple Support articles on heart health notifications and instructions for using irregular heart rhythm notifications.

HEART HEALTH MONITORING

With your Apple Watch, you can take care of your heart health. It keeps an eye on your heart rate and can send you alerts when it detects unusual patterns. For example, if your heart rate stays too high or too low for at least 10 minutes during a period of inactivity, your Apple Watch will alert you.

You can enable heart rate notifications when you first launch the Heart Rate app or at any other time.

In cases where your Apple Watch identifies an irregular heart rhythm, which could indicate the presence of atrial fibrillation (AFib), it will alert you promptly. If you've previously been diagnosed with atrial fibrillation, your Apple Watch helps you track the frequency of arrhythmia episodes and monitors certain lifestyle factors that may be affecting your condition.

RECEIVING HIGH OR LOW HEART RATE NOTIFICATIONS
1. Go to the Settings app on your Apple Watch.
2. Select "Heart."
3. Tap "High Heart Rate Notifications" or "Low Heart Rate Notifications."
4. Set the desired threshold.
5. Alternatively, on your iPhone, go to the Watch app, select "My Watch," and then tap "Heart Rate." Choose "High Rate" or "Low Rate" and configure the threshold.

MEDICATION TRACKING WITH APPLE WATCH
You can effectively manage your medications, vitamins, and supplements through the health app on your iPhone or iPad. On your Apple Watch, in the Medications app, you have the option to track your medications and improve them with reminders.

Note: The Medications app and its features should not be considered a substitute for medical advice. While you can access more information about the medications you are taking, it is crucial to consult with a doctor before making any health-related decisions.

SET MEDICATION SCHEDULES ON YOUR IPHONE OR IPAD
1. Open the Health app on your iPhone or iPad.
2. Choose one of the following options:
   - On iPhone: Tap Browse, then select Medications.
   - On iPad: Tap the sidebar, then tap Medications.
3. Tap "Add Medication" (for initial list creation) or "Add a medication" (to add to an existing list).
4. To find the medication, you can:
   - Type their name: Enter their name in the search field and tap Add.
   - In the US, you'll get suggestions as you type. You can select a suggestion or continue typing the name, then tap "Add."

- Use your camera (U.S. only, available on iPhone SE 2nd generation and later, iPhone XS, iPhone XR, and later): Tap the Camera button next to the search field and follow the onscreen instructions.
- If the medication isn't found, tap Search by Name, then enter the name as described above.
5. Follow the on-screen instructions to specify the type of medication, dosage, and if desired, create a custom image and schedule.
6. When you're done, tap "Close."

MEDICATION REGISTRATION

By default, Apple Watch will send reminders based on the schedule you set in the Health app on your iPhone or iPad. To register your medications:
1. If you receive a medication log notification, tap it.
2. Or open the Medications app on your Apple Watch.

For example, if you're asked to log your morning medications:
1. Tap on your current medication schedule for the morning.
2. Tap "Record All Footage."
3. Apple Watch will record your dosage, the number of units taken, and the time the medication was taken.

To log medications individually, scroll down, tap "Taken" under a medication, then tap "Done."
The Medications app will display the name of the medication and the time recorded under "Record."
To change the status of a registered medication, tap it, select "Taken" or "Skipped," then tap "Done."

ACCESS TO MEDICATION HISTORY

To view your medication history, go to the health app on your iPhone or iPad. On your iPhone, go to "Browse" and select "Medications." On your iPad, open the health app, tap the sidebar, and choose Medications.

ENABLING REMINDER CONTROLS AND IMPORTANT ALERTS

In addition to receiving alerts to log your medications, you can choose to receive a reminder if a medication has not been recorded 30 minutes after the scheduled time. In addition, you can enable important alerts for individual medications. These important alerts will appear on the lock screen and produce an audible sound, even when Full Silent Mode is turned on or the sound is muted.
Here's how to set it up:
1. Open the Health app on your iPhone or iPad.
2. Select one of the following options:
   - On iPhone: Tap Browse, then Medications.
   - On iPad: Tap the sidebar, then tap Medications.
3. Tap "Options" at the bottom of the screen.
4. Enable "Check Reminders".
5. To receive important alerts, tap "Important Alerts," then enable them for specific medications by tapping the corresponding buttons and selecting "Allow."
6. To turn off all important alerts, go to "Settings" on your iPhone or iPad, then go to "Health" > "Notifications." Locate the toggle next to "Important Alerts."

PARTICIPATE IN MINDFULNESS SESSIONS WITH YOUR APPLE WATCH

The Mindfulness app on your Apple Watch is designed to encourage daily practices of concentration, relaxation, and breathing exercises, fostering a sense of well-being and mindfulness in your routine. This app also incorporates a Mood feature, which allows you to engage in self-reflection about your emotional state.
A notable feature of the Mindfulness app is its integration with Apple Fitness+. With an Apple Fitness+ subscription, you can access guided meditation sessions right on your Apple Watch. These sessions can help you achieve deeper levels of relaxation and mindfulness, helping you manage stress and improve your overall mental health.

In addition, the app offers flexibility in terms of session customization. You have the option to customize the duration and settings of the sessions according to your preferences. This allows you to tailor your mindfulness practice to your specific needs and schedules.

During mindfulness sessions, the app monitors your heart rate, providing real-time feedback on physiological responses. This heart rate data can be invaluable for tracking your progress and understanding how different mindfulness exercises affect your body.

For added convenience, you can create a dedicated Breath watch face. This watch face offers quick and easy access to mindfulness exercises, making it easy to incorporate mindfulness moments into your day, no matter how busy you are.

The Mood feature within the app allows you to document your emotional state over time. You can record your mood in the moment or monitor your mood throughout the day, allowing you to gain insight into your emotional well-being and identify patterns or triggers.

To further explore and revise your mindfulness journey, the Mindfulness app integrates with Apple Fitness+. Completed guided meditation sessions are accessible and reviewed not only on your Apple Watch, but also on your iPhone, iPad, or Apple TV. This cross-device accessibility ensures that you can engage with your mindfulness practice wherever you feel most comfortable.

In summary, the Mindfulness app on Apple Watch is a comprehensive tool for incorporating mindfulness practices into your daily life. It offers guided meditation sessions, session customization, heart rate monitoring, mood recording, and cross-device accessibility, all aimed at improving your mental well-being and promoting a mindful lifestyle.

TRACK YOUR SLEEP WITH APPLE WATCH

Using the Sleep app on Apple Watch, you can create a sleep schedule to help you reach your sleep goals and gain insights into your sleep patterns. Here's how to use this feature:

OVERVIEW OF SLEEP TRACKING

1. With the Sleep app on Apple Watch, you can plan and track your sleep routines to reach your sleep goals.
2. As you wear your Apple Watch while sleeping, it tracks the time spent in different sleep stages, including REM, Main, and Deep sleep, as well as the number of awakenings.
3. When you wake up in the morning, open the Sleep app to check your sleep duration and review your sleep trends over the past 14 days.
4. If your Apple Watch has less than 30% battery power before bedtime, you'll get a reminder to charge it. You can quickly check the remaining charge in the morning.
5. To receive sleep data, your Apple Watch must track your sleep for at least four hours each night.

CREATING DIFFERENT SLEEP ROUTINES

You can set various sleep routines based on your preferences, such as different times for weekdays and weekends. Each procedure includes the following options:

1. Sleep duration goal.
2. Bedtime and wake-up times.
3. Alarm bell.
4. Activation of Sleep Full Immersion, which minimizes distractions at bedtime and protects sleep at night.

HOW TO SET UP SLEEP ON APPLE WATCH

1. Open the Sleep app on your Apple Watch.
2. Follow the on-screen instructions to set up your sleep schedule.
3. Alternatively, you can open the health app on your iPhone, select "Browse," then tap "Sleep," and finally choose "Start" under "Set Up Sleep."

CHANGE OR ADD YOUR BEDTIME

1. Open the Sleep app on your Apple Watch.
2. Tap the "Alarm" button.
3. Turn the Digital Crown to access "All Time."
4. Depending on your preference, you can change your existing bedtime by tapping on the current time or add a new bedtime by selecting "Add Now."
5. You can also adjust your sleep goal and relaxation time within this menu.
6. Sleep Full Focus turns off your Apple Watch screen to minimize distractions before your scheduled bedtime.
7. To manage these settings, you can tap your schedules, choose when it should be "Always On," change your sleep and wake times, adjust your alarm settings, remove or cancel your bedtime, and more.

CHANGING SLEEP OPTIONS

1. Open the Settings app on your Apple Watch.
2. Tap Sleep, then adjust the following settings:
   - "Wake Up on Relax": This option controls whether Sleep Full Focus turns on automatically when you wind down, or if you prefer to manage it manually in Control Center.
   - Sleep Screen: Simplify your Apple Watch screen and iPhone lock screen to reduce distractions.
   - Show Time: Displays the date and time on iPhone and Apple Watch when Focus is on.
   - You can also enable or disable sleep analytics and charging reminders. Sleep analytics tracks your sleep patterns and stores the data in the health app on your iPhone. Charging reminders ask you to charge your Apple Watch before charging time and notify you when it's fully charged.
   - You can adjust these sleep settings on your iPhone as well. Open the Watch app, tap "My Watch," and select "Sleep."

REVIEW OF SLEEP DATA

1. To see how much sleep you've got, open the Sleep app on your Apple Watch. It displays the number of hours you slept last night, the time spent in each sleep stage, and the average sleep duration over the past 14 days.
2. You can also view your sleep data on your iPhone by opening the health app, selecting "Browse," and choosing "Sleep." For more details, such as the average time spent at each sleep stage, tap "Show more sleep data."

RESPIRATORY RATE MONITORING

1. Apple Watch can help you track your breathing rate while you sleep, providing you with valuable insights into your health.
2. To access this information, open the health app on your iPhone, tap "Browse," and select "Respiratory System." From there, tap on "Respiratory Rate" and then "Show More Data - Respiratory Rate".
3. The Sleep section shows the range of your breathing rate during sleep. Please note that respiratory rate measurements are not intended for medical purposes.

DISABLING RESPIRATORY RATE MEASUREMENT

To turn off respiratory rate measurement on Apple Watch:
Open the Settings app on your Apple Watch.
Go to "Privacy & Security" > "Health."
Tap Breathing Rate, then turn it off.
Alternatively, you can disable it through the Watch app on your iPhone:
Open the Watch app on your iPhone.
Tap "Apple Watch", select "My Apple Watch".

Choose "Privacy" and turn off your breathing rate.
Apple Watch Series 8 or Series 9 can monitor your wrist temperature while you sleep, providing health information. To set it up:
In the Sleep app, enable "Track Your Sleep with Apple Watch."
Wear your Apple Watch while you sleep to establish a baseline temperature (takes a few nights).
You can check your wrist temperature in the health app on iPhone:
Open the Health app.
Go to "Browse", select "Body Measurements" and tap "Pulse Temperature".
Tap a data point on the chart for specific details.
To disable wrist temperature monitoring:

Go to the Settings app on your Apple Watch.
Go to "Privacy & Security" > "Health."
Tap "Wrist Temperature" and turn it off.
Alternatively, you can disable it through the Watch app on your iPhone:
Open the Watch app.
Select "My Watch", tap "My Apple Watch".
Go to the Privacy section and turn off wrist temperature monitoring.
Note: Wrist temperature monitoring is not a medical device and is not intended for medical diagnosis or treatment.

5- MANAGING CONTACTS ON APPLE WATCH

In the Contacts app, you can effectively manage your contacts on your Apple Watch. Here are the various actions you can take:

VIEWING CONTACTS
1. Open the Contacts app on your Apple Watch.
2. Use the Digital Crown to scroll through your contacts.
3. Tap a contact to view their photo. Scroll down to access additional details such as your email address, home and work addresses, and more.
4. To access the contact card, tap your photo in the top right corner.

COMMUNICATION WITH CONTACTS
1. In the Contacts app on your Apple Watch, use the Digital Crown to navigate through your contacts.
2. Select a contact and perform one of the following actions:
   - Tap the Phone button to view the contact's phone number and start a call.
   - Tap the Message button to open an existing message thread or create a new one.
   - Tap the More Options button, then select the Email button to compose a new email.
   - Tap the "More Options" button, and if you have Walkie-Talkie enabled, you can use the Walkie-Talkie button to invite someone to use Walkie-Talkie or start a conversation with someone who has already accepted the invitation.

CREATING A NEW CONTACT
1. Open the Contacts app on your Apple Watch.
2. Tap the Add button.
3. Enter the contact's name and, if applicable, their company.
4. Add your phone number, email address, and address as needed. Tap the checkbox to save the contact.

SHARE, EDIT, BLOCK, OR DELETE A CONTACT
1. Open the Contacts app on your Apple Watch.
2. Scroll through your contacts using the Digital Crown.
3. Tap a contact, scroll down, and choose one of the following actions:
   - To share a contact, tap the Share button in the bottom right, then select a sharing option.
   - To edit a contact, tap the Edit button, make the necessary changes, and tap "Remove" below a field to delete it.

- To block a contact, tap Block Contact.
- To delete a contact, tap Delete Contact.

VIEW A FRIEND'S LOCATION USING APPLE WATCH

The Find People app is a useful tool for locating and sharing your location with your important contacts. If your friends and family use iPhone, iPad, or Apple Watch and share their location with you, you can easily track them on a map to see where they are. You can also set up notifications to alert you when they depart or arrive at specific locations. For details on setting up the Find app on iPhone, see the iPhone User Guide.
Note: Find My app availability may vary by region.

ADDING A FRIEND

1. Launch the Find People app on your Apple Watch.
2. Scroll down and tap "Share My Location."
3. Use the Dictation, Contacts, or Keypad option to select a friend.
4. Choose an email address or phone number for your friend.
5. Specify how long you want your location to be shared: one hour, until the end of the day, or indefinitely.
6. Your friend will receive a notification that you've shared your location. They can choose to reciprocate by sharing their location with you. Once they've agreed to share their location, you can view it by going to a list or map in the Find My app on your iPhone, iPad, Mac, or the Find People app on your Apple Watch.

TO STOP SHARING YOUR LOCATION WITH A FRIEND

1. Tap your friend's name on the Find People screen.
2. Then, tap on "Stop Sharing."

VIEWING YOUR FRIENDS' LOCATIONS

1. Open the Find People app on your Apple Watch to see a list of your friends, their approximate locations, and the distance between you and each friend. Use the Digital Crown to scroll and view other friends.
2. Tap a friend to see their location on a map, including an approximate address.
3. To return to the friends list, simply tap on the back button located in the top left corner.

Alternatively, you can use Siri by saying "Where's Julie?"

NOTIFY YOUR FRIENDS OF YOUR DEPARTURE OR ARRIVAL

Launch the Find People app on your Apple Watch.

1. Tap your friend's name, then scroll down and tap "[Friend's Name] Notification."

2. On the next screen, enable "Notify [friend's name]" and choose whether to notify your friend when you leave your location or when you arrive at their location.

<u>**GET NOTIFICATIONS ABOUT YOUR FRIEND'S LOCATION**</u>
1. Open the Find People app on your Apple Watch.
2. Tap your friend's name, then scroll down and tap "Notify Me."
3. Turn on the "Notify Me" option and select whether you want to receive alerts when your friend leaves their location or when they arrive at your location.

SHARE YOUR LOCATION IN MESSAGES ON APPLE WATCH

In an iMessage conversation within the Messages app, you have the option to inform others about your current location by sharing it.
Note: Location sharing in Messages may not be available in all regions.

<u>**ENABLING "SHARE MY LOCATION"**</u>
1. Open the Settings app on your Apple Watch.
2. Tap Privacy & Security, then select "Location."
3. Make sure the "Share My Location" option is enabled. Scroll down, tap "Messages," and make sure one of the options: "Ask next time," "When I share," or "While using the app" is selected.

You can also access this setting on your paired iPhone. Go to Settings > Privacy & Security > Location Services > Share My Location. In the Location Services section, tap "Messages" and choose your preferred setting.

<u>**AUTOMATIC LOCATION SHARING AND UPDATING**</u>
When you share your location in Messages, you can choose to receive real-time updates within the conversation.
1. Open the Messages app on your Apple Watch.
2. Start composing a new message or open an existing conversation. Tap the Apps button, then select the Find My button.
3. Choose whether you want to share your location in real-time (updated in real-time) or as a static point.
   - For real-time sharing: Tap Share.
   - For static sharing: Tap the Pin button, then select Send Pin.
4. If you choose to share your real-time location, tap "Share" and decide how long you want to share your location:
   - Select "Forever" if you want to share your location until you manually stop sharing.
   - Tap "Send" to send the message (you can cancel if you change your mind).

The recipient can tap the message with the shared location to view it in the Maps app.
5. To share their location in response, the recipient can select the message with the location, which will open it in the Find People app, then tap "Share."

STOP SHARING LOCATION
1. Open the Messages app on your Apple Watch.
2. Join a conversation that includes the message where you shared your location.
3. Tap Stop Sharing.

Alternatively, open the Find People app, select the person you're sharing your location with, scroll down, and choose "Stop Sharing."

REQUEST SOMEONE ELSE TO SHARE YOUR LOCATION
1. Open the Messages app on your Apple Watch.
2. Start composing a new message or open an existing conversation.
3. Tap the Apps button, then select the Find My button.
4. Tap "Request."
5. Tap "Send" to send the message.

The other person will receive a message asking them to share their location, and the sharing will begin once you choose "Share."

6 - MANAGE YOUR WALLET ON APPLE WATCH

The Wallet app is a convenient tool for consolidating your credit cards and tickets in one accessible place. Wallet offers space for various items, including:
1. Cards for Apple Pay, such as Apple Card and Apple Cash. You can find instructions on how to set up Apple Pay on Apple Watch.
2. Transit cards, details on how to use them can be found in Using transit cards on Apple Watch.
3. Digital keys, which allow you to unlock your car or access your home or hotel room using keys stored in your Wallet on Apple Watch.
4. Driver's licenses or ID cards. You can learn more about using your driver's license or ID card in Wallet on your iPhone and Apple Watch (available in the U.S. only).
5. Student cards, which are contactless tickets, keys, badges, or ID cards.
6. Gift cards, boarding passes, and event tickets. Instructions on how to add and redeem passes in Wallet on Apple Watch can be found here.
7. Vaccination records, with information about using COVID-19 vaccination fact sheets on Apple Watch.

With Wallet on your Apple Watch, you can conveniently access and manage these important items.

APPLE PAY MADE EASY ON YOUR APPLE WATCH

Apple Pay offers a convenient, secure, and private payment method on your Apple Watch. After you add cards to the Wallet app on your iPhone and sync them to your Apple Watch, you can use Apple Pay in the following ways:
1. Contactless payments and apps: Make purchases in stores that support contactless payments and within Apple Pay-enabled apps using the credit, debit, and prepaid cards saved in the Wallet app.
2. Person-to-person payments: Send money easily and securely through Messages or using Siri.
3. Transit cards: You can include transit cards, which will be visible at the top of the Wallet app library, above the tickets.

By setting up Apple Pay through the Watch app on your iPhone, you can even make in-store purchases without your iPhone being present. Note that Apple Pay may not be available in all regions.

It's essential to remember that if you unpair your Apple Watch or disable passcode protection, you won't be able to use Apple Pay and any cards stored in your Wallet will be removed. If you turn off wrist tracking, you'll need to enter the passcode every time you use Apple Pay.

ADD A CARD TO YOUR APPLE WATCH USING IPHONE
1. Launch the Watch app on your iPhone.
2. Tap My Watch, then select Wallet & Apple Pay.
3. If you have cards linked to other Apple devices or recently removed cards, tap "Add" next to the card you want to include. Enter the card's CVV code when prompted.
4. For any other card, tap "Add Card" and follow the on-screen instructions carefully.
5. Keep in mind that your card issuer may require additional verification steps to confirm your identity.

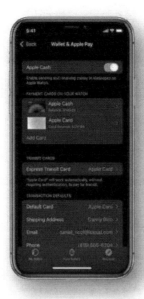

ADD A CARD DIRECTLY TO YOUR APPLE WATCH
1. On your Apple Watch, open the Wallet app.
2. Tap the More Options button, then select Add Card.
3. Choose from Apple Account, Debit or Credit Card, or Transit Card and follow the onscreen instructions.

SETTING A DEFAULT TAB
1. Open the Wallet app on your Apple Watch.
2. Tap the More Options button, then select Default Card.
3. Choose the desired card as the default.

Alternatively, on your iPhone, open the Watch app, tap "My Watch," then "Wallet & Apple Pay." Here you can select "Default Card" and make your choice or remove a card.

REORGANIZATION OF PAYMENT CARDS
To change the order of your payment cards, open the Wallet app on your Apple Watch. Touch and hold a card, then move it to the position you want.

REMOVE A CARD FROM APPLE PAY
1. Sign into the Wallet app on your Apple Watch.
2. Tap the card you want to remove.
3. Scroll down and select "Remove."

Alternatively, on your iPhone, open the Watch app, tap "My Watch," then "Wallet & Apple Pay." Choose the card you want to remove and tap "Remove Card."

LOST OR STOLEN APPLE WATCH:
If your Apple Watch is lost or stolen, follow these steps:
1. Turn on Lost Mode on your Apple Watch to prevent unauthorized payments.
2. Sign in to appleid.apple.com using your Apple ID and turn off card payments with Wallet.
3. In the "Devices" section, select your device and click "Remove Items" under Apple Pay.
4. Don't forget to contact your card issuers for further assistance.

MAKE PURCHASES WITH YOUR APPLE WATCH

MAKE IN-STORE PURCHASES
1. To make an in-store purchase with your Apple Watch, double-click the side button.
2. Swipe to select the desired card from the available ones.
3. Hold your Apple Watch a few inches away from the contactless reader, making sure the screen is facing the reader.
4. You will receive slight haptic feedback and hear a beep, confirming that your payment information has been transmitted.
5. Once the transaction is confirmed, you will receive a notification in the Notification Center.

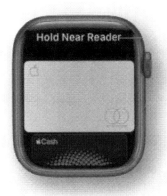

For cards that support this feature, you'll also receive purchase notifications for transactions made with any card added to your Wallet, even if you didn't use your Apple Watch, iPad, or iOS device to make the purchase. You have the option to disable notifications and transaction history for specific cards in your wallet. To do this, log in to the Watch app on your iPhone, tap "My Watch," proceed to "Wallet & Apple Pay," select a card, tap "Transactions," and toggle "Show History" and "Allow Notifications" on or off as needed.

MAKE IN-APP PURCHASES
1. To complete an in-app purchase on your Apple Watch, choose the "Apple Pay" option during the in-app checkout process.
2. Review your payment, shipping, and billing details.
3. To finalize the transaction, double-click the side button on your Apple Watch.

SEND, RECEIVE, AND REQUEST MONEY WITH APPLE WATCH (U.S. ONLY)
In addition to using Apple Cash for in-store purchases, you can conveniently send money to friends and family using your Apple Watch. It's a simple process, either through a message or with the help of Siri. You won't need anything else to send or request money.
Note: Apple Cash availability may vary by location. For complete information about using Apple Pay and Apple Cash, see the iPhone User Guide.

SEND A PAYMENT FROM APPLE WATCH

1. Use Siri: You can initiate a payment by saying "Send $25 to Clare." If you have multiple contacts named Clare, you'll be asked to select the correct person.
2. Open the Messages app on your Apple Watch.
3. Start a new conversation or select an existing one, then tap the Apps button followed by the Apple Cash button.
4. Use the Digital Crown or tap the plus and minus buttons to select an entire dollar amount.
5. If you need to send an amount with decimal places, such as $10.95, tap the entire amount, then tap the decimal space. Rotate the Digital Crown to choose the desired value.
6. Confirm by tapping "Send" and then double-click the side button to complete the transaction.

Once the payment is made, you will receive a confirmation message. Apple Cash Credit covers your payment, and if your Apple Cash balance is insufficient, the remaining amount is charged to your linked debit card.

CANCELING A PAYMENT

You can cancel a payment until the recipient accepts it.

1. Open the Wallet app on your Apple Watch.
2. Select a card and scroll through the list of transactions.
3. Tap the unpaid transaction, then select "Cancel Payment."

Alternatively, you can open the Watch app on your iPhone, tap "My Watch," go to "Wallet & Apple Pay," select your Apple Cash card, tap "Transactions," choose the unpaid transaction, and then tap "Cancel Payment."

REQUEST A PAYMENT FROM APPLE WATCH

You can request a payment using Siri or a message.

1. Using Siri: Say, "Ask Nico to send me $30."
2. Send a message: Open Messages on your Apple Watch, start a new conversation or select an existing one, tap the Apps button, followed by the Apple Cash button. Swipe left on the Send button, enter an amount, and tap "Request."

When you use Apple Cash for the first time, you'll be asked to agree to the terms and conditions on your iPhone before receiving payments. Subsequent payments are typically accepted automatically, unless you choose to accept them manually. To change this setting, sign in to the Wallet app on your iPhone, tap your Apple Cash card, tap More Info, select Card Details, then choose Accept Payments Manually.

RESPOND TO A PAYMENT REQUEST ON APPLE WATCH

Tap the "Send" button when you receive a payment request in Messages. If necessary, use the Digital Crown or the on-screen buttons to adjust the amount. Confirm by tapping "Submit," then double-click the side button to complete the payment.

VIEWING TRANSACTION INFORMATION ON APPLE WATCH

1. View transactions in Messages: Open the Messages app on your Apple Watch and select the Apple Pay message to access a summary of the transaction.
2. View transactions in Wallet: Open the Wallet app on your Apple Watch, select a card, and swipe to see a list of transactions. For more details, select a transaction.

To view all Apple Cash transactions on your iPhone, open the Watch app, tap "My Watch," go to "Wallet & Apple Pay," tap your Apple Cash card, then select "Transactions." If you want to email a PDF of your Apple Cash transaction history, tap your Apple Cash card, tap "Transactions," scroll down, and tap "Request Transaction List."

USE TRANSIT CARDS WITH APPLE PAY ON APPLE WATCH

You can use transit cards with Apple Pay on your Apple Watch to conveniently pay fares. Set a preferred card for quick payments in the Settings app. Hold your Apple Watch close to the reader to pay.

Unlock your car, house, or hotel door with keys in Apple Wallet:

Store your car, house, or hotel room keys safely in your wallet.

Unlock, lock and start your car with compatible devices (Series 6 or later).

Unlock your home with a compatible smart lock.

Open your hotel room door with keys in Apple Wallet from the hotel app.

Step-by-step instructions can be found in Apple Support articles. Availability may vary by region and device compatibility.

IPHONE 15 SENIORS GUIDE

APPLE WATCH

COLOR VERSION

7 - CLEANING AND MAINTENANCE

Keep your Apple Watch, band, and wrist clean and dry, especially after workouts.
Rinse water-resistant models with warm tap water after swimming.

1. To clean:
   - Spegni Apple Watch.
   - Remove the strap.
   - Use a non-abrasive, lint-free cloth, optionally moistened with fresh water.
   - Dry thoroughly.
2. Avoid cleaning when charging or using external heat sources.
3. Do not use household cleaners, ultrasonic equipment, or compressed air.
4. Do not insert objects into openings or doors.

Glass Surface:
1. Ion-X glass or sapphire crystal with oleophobic coating.
2. The coating wears out over time; Abrasive materials can scratch it.
3. Handle with care to avoid damage.

Buttons, Digital Crown, Connectors, and Ports:
1. Avoid applying excessive pressure or forcing connectors into ports.
2. Check for obstructions and ensure proper alignment.
3. Gently bend the cables to prevent them from fraying or breaking.
4. Inspect the cables and connectors regularly for damage.

Apple Watch Magnetic Charging Accessories:
1. Discoloration can occur due to dirt and debris; This is normal.
2. Wipe the surface with a non-abrasive, lint-free cloth to prevent damage.
3. Avoid the use of cleaning products.

Temperature:
1. Use Apple Watch between 0°C and 35°C; Store at a temperature between -20°C and 45°C.
2. Extreme temperatures can damage Apple Watch and affect battery life.
3. Drastic temperature changes should be avoided.
4. Temperature alerts can affect the functionality of the device in extreme conditions.

Magnets:
1. Keep access or credit cards away from Apple Watches, bands, and magnetic charging accessories.

These guidelines are essential for the proper functioning and lifespan of your Apple Watch. Please follow them carefully to ensure the longevity and safe use of the device.

8 - UNAUTHORIZED CHANGES TO WATCHOS

watchOS is designed to be secure and reliable from the moment the device is activated.

Its built-in security features protect your device from malicious software, viruses, and ensure secure access to personal and business data.

Unauthorized changes to watchOS, often known as jailbreaking, allow security features to be circumvented and can lead to several issues, including security risks, instability, and reduced battery life on the altered Apple Watch.

Security Risks:
1. Jailbreaking your device eliminates the layers of protective security that safeguard your personal information and Apple Watch.
2. This elimination of security measures exposes your personal data to potential hackers, device damage, network breaches, and the introduction of malware, spyware, or viruses.

Instability:
1. Unauthorized alterations can cause unexpected and frequent device crashes, application closures and freezes, as well as data loss.

Reduced battery life:
1. Modified software can accelerate battery drain, resulting in reduced battery life per charge for Apple Watch.

Voice & Data Reliability:
1. Unauthorized changes can result in dropped calls, unreliable or slow data connections, and inaccurate or delayed location data.

Service Interruptions:
1. Services such as iCloud, iMessage, FaceTime, Apple Pay, Visual Voicemail, Weather, and Stocks may be compromised or stop working on your device.
2. Third-party apps that rely on Apple's push notification service may face difficulties in receiving notifications or receive notifications intended for other compromised devices.
3. Other push notification-based services, such as iCloud and Exchange, may have trouble synchronizing data with their respective servers.

CONCLUSION

This comprehensive index provides a detailed guide to effectively utilize and manage the features of the Apple Watch Ultra. The content is systematically organized, starting with the initial setup and connection process, addressing potential issues during pairing, and extending to advanced functionalities and health features. Users can efficiently navigate through the instructions, covering various aspects such as customization, app management, communication, health monitoring, and more.

The index reflects a holistic approach to using the Apple Watch Ultra, ensuring that users can seamlessly integrate the device into their daily lives. Whether it's setting up multiple watches, adjusting preferences, managing notifications, or exploring health and fitness features, the index covers a wide range of topics. Additionally, it emphasizes the practical aspects of using the device, such as making calls, handling notifications, and even managing wallet features like Apple Pay.

The inclusion of sections on cleaning, maintenance, and addressing unauthorized changes to WatchOS highlights the importance of proper care and security considerations for the Apple Watch Ultra. Overall, this index serves as a valuable resource for both beginners and experienced users, offering a step-by-step guide to maximize the functionality and utility of the Apple Watch Ultra.

Made in the USA
Monee, IL
30 October 2024